THE
COURSE
OF THE
SEEKER

THE COURSE OF THE SEEKER

OMAR ALI-SHAH

TALE WEAVER
PUBLISHING

LOS ANGELES

Tale Weaver Publishing wishes to thank the author, Omar Ali-
Shah, for his assistance and guidance and Augey Hayter for his
dedication in seeing this book come to written form.

Many thanks also to the invaluable assistance and determination
of the members of the Western Institute for their perseverance in
proofing, transcribing and typing the manuscript.

Front cover by Wong Design

Front cover photography by Levon Parian

Library of Congress Catalog Card Number 88-050953

Includes bibliography

ISBN 0-942139-07-0

Send Inquiries to:
Tale Weaver Publishing, Inc.
636 N. Robertson Blvd.
Los Angeles, California 90069

CONTENTS

EDITOR'S NOTE

With the exception of the Introduction the following chapters have not been written: all are lightly edited transcriptions of discourses by the Sayed Omar Ali-Shah which were taped when talking to Sufi study groups, mostly between 1985 and 1987. We felt it was best to retain the informal and improvisational nature of the discourse form, rather than to try and transform these talks into formal treatises. What this method of making a book may lose in literary merit, it gains in accuracy: this is a completely precise record of how Agha, as his pupils call him, talks to his people.

None of the chapters here have been added to, or "improved" in any way, and we have tried to limit the editing to minimal tightening and clarification of things which are out of place when seen in a written text (split infinitives, stops and starts, etc.) as well as references to contexts which would take too long to explain.

This whole book is, in fact, Agha thinking on his feet — in the time I have known him I have never seen him read out a prepared speech, and although he'll make intelligent use of pauses for laughter, I have never once seen him use actor's tricks to ingratiate himself with an audience.

Communicating what actually happens in the Tradition between teacher and pupil is extraordinarily difficult, because if you talk to a hundred people you will get a hundred different stories of how something revealed itself to them — a general framework exists, but acquiring awareness is necessarily a personal process and can never be reduced to an all-encompassing equation. One of the great subtleties of the Sufi Tradition is the way in which the teaching communicates itself to the requirements of each individual while remaining constant over a time-span of many generations; it can do this only because the teaching takes place through contact with a living teacher of the Tradition, rather than limiting itself to cruder tools like books, theories, and rudderless groupings of well-wishers.

If you look at a snapshot, it is up to you to read the image. A book like this, although valuable as a document and as an indication, is only part of the story — the rest of the story will always have to be filled in by the individual circumstances and perception involved.

In the Tradition, it is the seeker who forgoes his or her own missing links, using the teacher and the companions for guidance, and cementing the edifice with trust. This book is a document, no more, no less, and faithfully represents a Sufi teacher in the eighties in certain contexts — the rest is up to you.

Augy Hayter

INTRODUCTION

In the West, there is much confusion, much misunderstanding, concerning the Sufi Tradition of teaching and the inner development of the individual. The Sufi Tradition is, as it has always been, an exact science, not to be lumped together with a myriad of "isms" that besmirch much popular philosophy.

The Tradition, as we who were born in it, teach it, and represent it, is not a hybrid doctrine, though many Western commentators have sought to prove its Greek roots. The Tradition was developed by men of skill, dedication and foresight – men who overcame political, social, cultural, and physical barriers in an incessant search for the knowledge that would enable mankind to develop.

Early Sufi Saints and mystics sought to teach, to write, and to compose verse to offer back to man the esoteric knowledge that established religion no longer could offer. The founding fathers of Sufi thought came up against the constant opposition of Establishment figures during their lives. Their writings and their verse have outlived those who accused them of "heresy" and worse.

They identified the need in man. They identified the yearning, not for more and more words and comfort, but for a teaching that would transcend time and place, races and religions, pride and prejudice. The noble roll-call of Teachers in the Tradition includes such names as al-Ghazzali, Hafiz, Jami, Saadi, Salman i-Farsi, Omar Khayyam, Rumi, al-Beiruni, who are but a few luminaries whose works have received wide acclaim throughout the world.

These men, as they did during their lives, shunned the limelight and applause of the Establishment and the intellectuals – their task was to build, and build they did. With their books, poetry, and wisdom, they laid the foundation-stones of the living philosophy, which those outside the Tradition call "Sufism."

Their motive, their mission, was to delineate such a path, that man, once safely on it, could aspire to a higher and permanent consciousness, in which state he could safely hope to understand himself and his relation with his God.

This path is not for all, for it is not all roses and violins — it is an uphill task, fraught with confusion as man struggles with his conditioning, but it is a path full of warmth, full of light, and full of love.

Those of us who have been fortunate enough to have been born in or to have joined the Tradition, say to all: open and read these pages, there may be a way for you.

Omar Ali-Shah
Surrey, England
August, 1988

The Sufi tradition knows no frontiers. It is a tradition that has existed in the hearts and minds of men from the earliest years of Eastern civilisation. Because of its Eastern background some have considered it to be "just another Eastern cult." Sufism is neither a cult nor a religion: it is a practical philosophy based on tried and proven techniques. It is, as history has shown, easily assimilated into Western culture because its basic truths are universally recognised and only its technique different. Yet is this difference of technique a handicap? The answer is no because such techniques as are used by Sufi teachers in the West do not demand activities that are incompatible with Western life.

To work in the Sufi tradition in the West a person must make a commitment to themselves; take on the responsibility for their thoughts and actions in a very much deeper way than they might have been taught. It does not imply that they must reject or scorn Western values or attitudes, many of which are valid and useful. It does mean that a student of the Sufi path must develop, and be satisfied with other, new terms of reference by which he measures himself, others and slowly, his awareness of God.

Sufis say that a traveller on this path must be "in the world but not of the world." This does not mean being "unworldly". Unworldliness in this Century is out of place and out of step and the "unworldly" end up being out of a job too.

The Sufi tradition leads man to a realisation of himself and, hopefully, to a deeper understanding of how he stands in relation to God and how he can approach Him.

If you, Reader, are contemplating entering this path, welcome.

Syed Omar Ali-Shah
Naqshband.

Chapter 1

ANSWERING QUESTIONS ABOUT THE TRADITION

Function of questions because study course is not fixed; Using texts as constants and how they connect to personal nature of student; How the effort to formulate a question can enable the questioner to find the relevant answer.

I don't at all mind answering questions. I'm not specifically inviting them in the sense that one must ask a question and therefore formulate one; but one of the things is that at an early stage of contact with the Tradition, there are naturally some questions which are brought up and which come up. Some are very similar or have the same basis. Some questions are just for clarifying certain points: and since there is no fixed course or schedule of study, there are obviously texts which we use; and during the course of study one does refer people to certain texts to read or to use.

However, part of the Teaching is and has to be of a personal nature, in the sense that certain texts or activities or exercises are suggested to people as individuals; *because it is a necessary function of the Tradition that a person's individual characteristics, problems, energies, capacities and so forth, should be allowed for within the context of the Tradition, and within their capacity to use them.*

So it's no good saying "Okay, go off and read Jami, Hafiz, Saadi, Rumi" hoping that the person will hit on something which is useful to them. There is so much, or too much, hit-and-miss type of thing – all-or-nothing type of activity – it causes confusion and it causes people to get despondent. They blame themselves, they blame the technique, they blame somebody else, and of course, everything ends in tears.

In the Teaching, the degree of, as it were, personal tuition applies, in the sense that contact is kept up so that the person who is teaching can monitor the various stages of perception, or being, or whatever you like to

*call it, of the person; and indicate to them at what specific time they should
do what particular activity.*

Those textbooks and other things are available and are referred to
from time to time, but since there are no set rules: "1 2 3 4 do this, afterwards do that" and so on, en masse, en bloc, that one can refer to — it
is often useful for a person to clarify to themselves, their position, their
intention; hence to one stage or another or at different stages. So as I
say from time to time one invites questions: not, again, with the intention of galvanizing people into tremendous activity: "I must find a question for next Thursday" or something like that.

If there is a question, certainly it could be and can be put, not always at a specific time, in the sense that "every fourth Monday in the
month, every third Thursday after x" or whatever, there is a question-
and-answer session — no. Sometimes, more often than not, I talk all the
time — sometimes, very infrequently, I allow other people to talk for one
or two minutes and then I start talking all over again, but the teaching
technique does allow for the question and answer, for the simple
reason, that sometimes in formulating a question which is relevant, they
are more often than not in possession of the factors that will give them
the answers. And in formulating it, they very often find the answer.

But that is not to say it is inevitable, that's not to say that a person
should desperately formulate the question on the assumption that they
will inevitably find the answer. They may do so; if they don't, then putting the question is still a valid thing and it is encouraged because there
are areas of complexity or confusion, and as long as the question is not
what I call a "show-off" question, i.e., a person has rushed off and read
an obscure tract by somebody, and comes and says: "I seem to remember that Al-Halka said that the cause of all illness was the Euphrates
and what do I do about that and do I do anything?"

This is a very complex question, and it's a tribute to their research
and capacity, but unless they want to get an equally ridiculous and
garbled answer from me, it is advisable not to ask it. If it is a question,
which is a problem, is something which also a person feels, that might
be beneficial to other people in the group, then they can possibly ask
it.

If the question is too wide or too deep, "What is the meaning of
life?" or "What is this, that and the other thing?" — then again I don't

think that the person will necessarily get an answer, whether I know it or not. I only answer questions if in my judgment a person, and the people listening will benefit from the answer, and more importantly, will have the competence to understand the answer, otherwise it becomes another jargon, and they go off more confused, in fact, than when they started. So if a question tends to be more complex than necessary, I won't necessarily compliment them on their intellect by replying on that level; I may answer them on a very much lower, and in my estimation, a more comprehensible level.

So, any pertinent questions?

Q: This, what I would call instinct, is it significant to development in the Tradition ...

A: Instinct, or common sense or horse sense is a thing which unfortunately has become vastly underrated, because it's dismissed ... you know, people say "the person wears sensible shoes" or "sensible clothes" – it has slight implications of the fuddy-duddy. They very often don't even know what they mean when they're saying that, it always has a pejorative sense to it.

Now sense is, to us, a basic human reaction to situations, a form of analysis which is, I don't know how the Americans call it, a "gut reaction" or something like that. But this is selling it short. No matter how many degrees a person has, no matter how intellectual they might consider themselves to be, what is it, for instance, that wakes them up at night when they smell smoke? Race memory, Neanderthal man, this, that and the other thing, yes – but you don't dismiss it.

You hear people say, for instance, "my old grandmother, my old mother, my old aunt" used to do this, that and the other thing, or say this, that and the other thing – and then they'll laugh, they'll be sort of slightly shy or guilty or a bit silly. No, we hold that sense, the impression, the feeling that one gets from the person, the face, the situation, the thing – it should not be ignored. It has a definite function.

Most things which communicate or say something to the common sense of the person are things which are not capable of being measured, labeled, weighed – socially, politically, or in any other way put in a category. People say "Oh yes I felt something" or "It was a sensation" and very often people don't say that, because in this day and age, unfortunately, you get people who'll then say: "Well then, what was it? I

mean thick, or happy, or sad, or hot, or cold, or excited, or wet, or dry?"
And you say, "Well no, you know ..." and they say either "Oh yes" and
they call the men in white coats, or they say, "You don't want to talk to
him or her, because they're a bit off."

So this has been understood to the degree that people are reluctant or even ashamed to say anything in that area — they keep it to themselves. Sometimes they don't understand it themselves, and they get
worried about it and "Am I going mad?" or is this a genetic or race
thing or something like that, whereas we hold that this is one of the perfectly normal senses that the person has.

There are the five senses, and people say there is a sixth sense or
seventh sense and this, that and the other thing — why not? Why should
it be considered to be something which is incredibly sophisticated,
rarified, and somewhat supernatural — either fraught with danger so
don't touch it, or go overboard on it?

No, it is an instinct which is capable of being developed, and it is a
sense which we use within the Tradition to talk to and communicate
with, on levels which are not touched by the conventionally accepted
five senses. The effect on the person of, for instance, a micro-climatic
situation, is something which a person can't put a name to. And we say,
"Do you need to?" Must it be codified? Must it be labeled? If it is a useful thing, if it is something that feels good, must it necessarily be traced
down to something specific or something particular? Why can't it be
just accepted as being -"*Grug!*"- and either used or accepted?

If you have a wooly scarf and it keeps you warm, and somebody
says "Oh that's not Harrod's, that's British Home Stores" — is it any less
warm? The answer is, if you're sold upon Harrod's, yes, it becomes so
to you. But have you given your neck maybe the vote? No.

So the answer is: yes, very definitely, the six-sense unconscious-
self level, which has been called all sorts of things, is important and
should be given adequate attention along with other senses like the tactile; and if something by tactile examination appears hard or something
like that, you accept it as being, on the basis of experience, hard or soft
or whatever. You don't then examine it, you don't examine the tactile
with another of your senses, because the only judgment which is required on that particular things is: is this smooth enough or shall I polish
it some more?

You can listen to it or you can look at it till kingdom come, but it does not change the necessity that you have. When people start swapping things around, they get into error. Equally, if something appears, for whatever reason, basic horse sense, to be good or bad or capable of being looked at or useful, this is a thing which one does use and which one should work on and recognize within the Tradition.

One has to make a delicate, not a tremendous and fundamental examination—one has to make a slight difference between this sort of basic feeling and one's personal hangups, because that can easily happen, and people do confuse the two, and it can lead to complications.

Instinct is very often the deep consciousness, not the subconscious that people are talking about all the time—the deep consciousness communicating on a very human and basic level. Very often it's something nudging you in an unsophisticated way and calling your attention to something which possibly might appear hostile or alien, because you have measured it from other points of view.

Q: Does reaction or impulse differ basically from person to person?

A: Well, I think there are people who by personality and by nature are sort of, what one might call professional understanders or professional worriers.

They take it as a bit of a challenge, like sort of bits written down, and therefore "I must read it," therefore "I must understand it" and "I must use it."

Very often that feeling is followed by another thing: "I must do it now!" This is impatience, this is greed, and it can also be a result of education, conditioning, and terms of reference. "Unless you've learnt that book by the end of term, forget it," or you get punished, ask a question and learn all this book. This is the more familiar sort of conditioning, and people very often think they have a need to think and learn about everything altogether, all the time, on all levels. This is a very desirable situation, however there is such a thing as mental indigestion, you can take up too much. Everything you take up—useful information, pieces of practical information—is stored and is brought out at the right time. If you follow a technique, for instance, driving a car—it's stored. There's a known technique, you don't worry about it—when you have to drive a car you bring out that piece of memory and you use it.

If you have several different techniques which you are trying to remember all at the same time, and then you bring them all out, and you have to look through them to see which one you apply to drive the car — then you have a problem; *because the purpose of knowledge, of getting knowledge, is to be able to use it. It's not just to file it: "I have got so much knowledge."*

There is a story that, you know, the wise man who doesn't use his knowledge is like a donkey with a load of books. You can say "I've read so many books, I can't tell you" or you say to somebody "why don't you read this book?" and they say "I've read one." And neither extreme is correct.

You've learned something, a piece of knowledge or a technique; you allow enough of it, at the moment, to satisfy your requirements. You use that knowledge or technique at the same time as practising it a bit more, to increase your knowledge and also your capacity to use it — but you don't try and hold everything and, at the same time, you're examining it, trying to use it, trying to explain it to yourself. You have to be patient with yourself because the way knowledge is stored in the human brain is very sophisticated. It's not a question of volume. It's stored in wafer-thin layers.

You can have so much that — it's the old familiar thing, and I'm sure we've all done it, if you're looking for something, and you start looking through an old box of papers, you get to the fifth piece of paper in the tin, and your memory goes off on something else. This is a very familiar thing. *So it's all about trying to keep something, and bring it out and use it.*

When you work through all the terms of reference and things which you have, your search becomes confused, you're looking through lots and lots of files and trying to say "Does that apply to this?" and "Does that apply to that?" So what I'm saying, I'm afraid, is a horrific sort of thing from the practical and educational point of view — that is: *don't learn so much, but what you do learn, learn well, and be able to use it cor-rectly,* otherwise you get into the very familiar situation which some ladies have, which is when they fill their kitchens and larders with every-thing in case they might need it. It is a sort of greed, it's an aspect of greed. And coupled with that, if you have impatience — "I want to use this piece of knowledge," "I want to understand about that," — it is really a technique for amassing knowledge – and this again can lead to one's getting uptight and nervous, saying "Why aren't I using this?" or "Why can't I? What's wrong with me? I'm stupid," or something like that. And then you have the vicious circle.

You see, applied knowledge or applied technique in a context which is useful, is obviously much more worthwhile than any amount of theory.

It is a failure of some educational techniques that they fill a person with information. Now that is okay up to a point; you go to school and you come out at the age of sixteen or whatever, you have learnt hundreds of things which you only need for your final examinations at school. After that, you never use them; but you need them up to that point. After that point, you should have worked out what you want to do, either University or whatever.

So you can leave aside certain things which are unnecessary and gradually narrow down the area of education which you want to do. You don't take the whole lot with you all the time, because the feeling always is "Oh dear, there's a book, maybe I should read it now," or "When should I read it?" or "Should I be reading it?" or something like that. It is a form of greed, some people amass what is called information. Now, for facts: if it is in one's profession, or if it's in something that one needs facts, then one learns the facts which one applies to one's profession. Other things become what is called incidental information.

If there's a train which leaves from Paddington for Oxford every morning at 7:40, that is a fact. I don't necessarily have to remember that, or remember that there's one that leaves at 9:20 and there's one that leaves at 11:40 and there's one that leaves at 2:30, right? Those facts are only important to me if I regularly travel between London and Oxford, otherwise they're incidental information. If I need them, I can telephone the station or I can look it up in the book. I don't have to carry the timetable with me the whole time, nor do I have to carry all the London Telephone Directories with me all the time in case I might need them.

So the "in case, in case" thing is if there's only one telephone directory for London in the whole world; then of course you don't have to carry it with you, you set up a business. If you've got the only telephone directory in the world, you can make a fortune by telling people o' ¬r people's telephone numbers. But you don't carry all the information, and, because you've got it, plan to apply it.

So you must remember that in the Tradition which we have, everybody has started somewhere. All right, some people were born into it, some people have family associations with it, some people heard of it, some people knew people who were in it; and many people have read things about the Tradition, which, depending on the way they interpreted or heard about it or found it – have given it all sorts of names: good, bad, silly, unnecessary, and so forth.

But it is basically a teaching, and the purpose of it is to develop people by a series of techniques: hearing, reading, exercising – cutting out a lot of unnecessary, certainly, over-intellectualisations – because it is not so much a time factor, that one says "Well, one must now ... " or "We don't have enough time" or "We must push it."

Q: Why are people like that?

A: The answer to the question is that people don't have to be like that. They don't have to go through life confused, stumbling; they have the basic capacity to develop themselves; there are techniques – one of which happens to be the *Tradition* – which were put together very carefully, very clearly, *as a path* to be followed.

And I am committed to it, therefore I must obviously say that I think that it is a person's duty towards themselves to look for such a path and to find it.

If they are not prepared to be motivated by their own, call it personal interest, there is such a thing as what is called "intelligent self-interest." Intelligent self-interest is not greed, everybody has self-interest that is balanced – intelligent self-interest means that they are using a certain amount of intelligence to choose things, to think and to act in an intelligent way rather than in a reactive way.

There's a difference between instinctive and reactive. Instinctive is something which one feels, for instance, which suggests that this is reasonable, this isn't, and this is a bit dodgy. Reactive is a result of conditioning, and it's because of personality fixations or hangups that a person reacts in a way. Reactive is more a lack of thought. Somebody says something and you say "Why?" That isn't to say that you look at them for ten minutes and then say "Why" and everybody says "Well, it took a bit of a long time to sink in."

Again, there's a difference between the two; reactive tends to be as a result of some condition or attitude. Instinctive is something which is coming to the surface and is triggering off a feeling or a train of thought.

Nobody, and I mean nobody, wants to fall from one hole into another and that sort of thing. People don't do it deliberately in the sense that they see a puddle of water and they jump straight into it deliberately. It isn't even a considered judgment. It sometimes is "Oh well, I suppose I might as well jump into that hole." Now this doesn't do them any great credit, even on any basis. If their feet are on fire then it is indicated that they should jump into a puddle, but sort of "For want of anything better to do, oh I suppose I might as well do something ..." I mean it's the answer to that Mexican chap who jumped into a whole cactus, a big cactus with spikes, and they asked him afterwards "Why did you jump into the cactus?" And he said, "Well, it seemed a good idea at the time." Maybe that was a better choice if the alternative would have been jumping into a fire. But since the alternatives are never really quite as drastic as that — the lesser of two evils — people are endowed with capacities which they can develop if they know how, and there's no reason why they shouldn't do it.

I get angry with people when they don't take advantage of their capacity in any way. I don't often show it because it would demonstrate more openly my arrogance — the "I know, so therefore I am fed up with you, so why don't you do it?" — because inevitably, people also get fed up with this. But my function is to teach, and it will be done.

Pursuing people — we don't chase them up. We have a thing, as it were, an offer, a technique. The books are there, the tactics are there, the techniques are there, and, you know, we go on pushing, talking about it, offering, indicating it to people.

Don't think for a moment — you are not necessarily dunces — that this sort of thing: "It's all right for you" and "I was born in it and I was brought up in it" — in order to have a mandate to teach, one has to know, very fundamentally, not only what one is teaching, but the people one is teaching to, and understand what makes them tick.

Everybody would love anybody who teaches anything — but if a poor wretch sitting upstairs day after day listening to the children thumping away on a piano, and thinking "Should I have taken up anything else" — can you imagine, for instance, the dream of that unfortunate piano teacher, to go in and see a toddler who will sit down and play Beethoven from morning to night after being given one lesson? That is the dream of anybody who teaches anything. "You see, now you do this, and you do it like that, and you hold this, and you do like that," and the person does it immediately. "Good heavens, it's marvelous." Then you go mad, because the exaltation is too much.

So when you are dealing with a material, which in this case happens to be with human material, you have to know exactly what you're dealing with. If you expect people to learn or understand the music immediately, you're living in a Utopian world; it's no good to them, it's no good to you. You have to understand their shortcomings, problems, negativity, positivity, the up and downs, the whole thing, and use whichever technique applies to that situation.

So if a person has faults, I don't like the faults, or approve of them, but I can understand that they have them, and I can understand that they don't like them. It is not good enough for me to continue to say to them: "Well, you're like this" and "You're like that" and "Why don't you do this" and "Why don't you do that?" without telling them how to, because then it just becomes a sort of one-way criticism and after all, usually, people are very much critical of themselves, and they are fed up with criticism or confusion. The thing is I can go on like that, but I mean, so one says, okay, now this is not the way to the stars, this has no promises, no nothing, because people do the work. It doesn't sit with everybody, it perhaps is different, as people go along, from what they might have imagined it to be; but at the same time the intention is to develop people, allow them to develop and help them to develop to the point where they can use the energy and the capacity with which they were born and which they can develop.

Unless you give them contexts in which they can use it, situations in which they can use it; you have to — this is the term I use — you have to sheepdog, you know, bow wow wow, wow wow wow, and push them along. You glorify your sheepdog function — because nobody wants to be the sheep, do they?

One of the natural conditionings, or those reservations which have to be overcome, is the ever-present idea or suspicion or thought of a sort of cult situation. Now cults, per se, are good, bad, indifferent and pernicious — some of them. We claim very strongly that we are not a cult in the sense that there are no promise-menace questions. Basically a person is responsible to themselves. As I say, the teaching is there — they are getting flexibility within the teaching. They owe themselves a responsibility. They are not political or in any other way associated with anything except humanity — and this is not a sort of "Me, me, goodness of humanity" type of thing. I don't care particularly for humanity as such. The majority of humanity are slobs. But they can be pushed, pulled, shoved and developed if they once recognize they are slobs.

If they're happy to be slobs, I'm not going to go and flush them out and draft them in. I don't work on a head-count basis; if the people feel the necessity to look for something, it is available. If they're happy in their slobbovian way, then I am no sort of revivalist who says "The end of the world is nigh" and all that sort of thing.

This Teaching is a developmental technique and it demands discipline — self-discipline and tenacity, and a fair amount of good solid common sense — and also to detach the Teaching from the "paranormal" because it is very necessary, especially now with so many of these cults in this spooky, mysterious, supernatural, paranormal, crystal-ball business. This is a very precise technique.

It manifests itself in different and curious ways. When I say that it manifests itself in different ways it is, for instance, that you might do something or read something, and all of a sudden say "Good heavens, that's familiar" or "I understood it" or as they say, "Suddenly everything became wonderfully clear." Well, yes, not everything actually, but merely a little precise thing which might have been a little bit confused before, a bit unclear before, becomes clear. And at that point you can give everything or anybody the credit; but you can also tell yourself "I worked that out."

Also, there are limits, as I say, to that. You don't take all the credit because if you're not feeling so marvelous the next day, then you say "It was only silly old me who did it, and I've been a fool for years, therefore I couldn't really have done it and it wasn't worth it anyway. So you have to give the credit to the effort which you're put in, the energy which you have generated in a particular context — plus the Teaching — to produce the equation. If you add nothing to something, you still have the something, but if you add something to something you get a plus path. As I said before, we have every sort of technique which fits every sort of situation, and we apply them according to the demands of the person, the situation, the context — and it is so skillful because the fundamental basis has been worked out — therefore the permutations are innumerable, because they have one central basis.

When something happens as a result of doing something, it is not the sort of transcendental breakthrough — it breaks through in little areas. They can be of a physical satisfaction area, they can be an "Aha, I see" sort of thing, or "I think I see," some sort of taste, some sort of feeling — according to, obviously, the amount of prescience that a person can handle.

It is very easy — no it's not, fortunately — but theoretically it is, for a person to blow their top. As I say, it is not easy because there are safeguards, but if they did suddenly understand everything in the world or what have you, it would really frighten or confuse them more, rather than having it fed to them in reasonable doses.

It's not a stop-start. It's really a question of momentum. After all if you have a very large wheel — very heavy, very big — a mill-wheel; the initial energy to get that moving is very considerable. After which the rotation can be kept up at a certain minimum amount of energy. It can be spun a little bit faster, by a little bit more energy — but equally, not a constant and frenetic energy to keep it moving, because what is the speed of a wheel? How long is a piece of string? It has to be intimately geared and associated with that particular context or wheel, otherwise as I say, there is confusion.

It's an initial amount of energy, and then a constant raising of the amount of energy which is not dissipating, it is concentrating and it doesn't detract — the person is manufacturing and generating enough energy consonant with the speed of their wheel and consonant with the amount of extra energy they might need to push it a little faster — all the time a little faster.

It is a gradual activity, but again, what is gradual in terms of time — days, months, years — gradual according to the person. Hence, coming back to what I was saying at the very beginning, that is a personalised thing, in the sense that there is no great book of words which you look up. If there were, it would be even more confusing and probably dangerous, because if going over the words — 365 pages, one page for every day of the year — time changes. What you did on the 7th of November last year is probably not remotely associated with what you're going to do this year or next year. You may do exactly the same thing, but the one thing which will probably have changed is time, and the whole context thereof.

So a very dangerous thing is the sort of overall existence of a book of words. We're not dealing with that. There's a varying momentum of people in a group. So what does one do? If I say something, is it different to everybody? Well, not necessarily, because in that firstly I — as you have noticed — constantly repeat myself in sort of variations on a theme. Because though this is something fundamental, to be shared by everybody, yet I tend to put in the things which refer to people or which can stimulate them to a train of thought. So they go off, and they worry the bone — hopefully the bone, and not themselves.

Because if they worry themselves, i.e., "I didn't understand what that was about" and "what does this mean" and so forth and so on, they are chasing the phantom bone. But if they've got a bone which they have got to take away — possibly, not necessarily — and it's a tangible thing which they want to examine and relate to themselves — then this is useful — rather than going away and having to have constant recall of everything which was conceivably said in every particular relationship. This becomes, then, confusing.

You see, somebody once said — I think I did, in fact — that if you float into Trafalgar Square six feet off the ground, you get a million people. From scaffolders who want to kill you, because if you teach everybody, nobody needs scaffolds, or airline pilots who want to know how it's done, or whatever — everybody has a reason. They want to know how you did it for their own purposes, they don't want to know what went into doing it. So you say, "All right, if you're so marvelous go fly into Trafalgar Square and say the world is coming to this" — and everybody says "I want to learn to do this" — and it's a thoroughly disagreeable sensation in any case. If you wonder what they went through to do that, whether it's useful — by the time they do it, they don't want to do it.

Admittedly, any technique of this nature, i.e., the Tradition, has, as I say, certain overtones of "the East" and "mysterious things" and what have you and so forth. Well, they're not really mysterious at all. People say, for instance, "the paranormal" — no. You can call it, for instance, "supernormal" the "normal normal" — paranormal is really, at this stage, too exalted a step. "Supernatural" — again, the word has already become old-fashioned, because everything is "fantastic." I mean if you talk like this, it means it's from fantasy, therefore it's unreal — no.

More than the normal — the normal state of the person is not the horrid, depressed, abominable, confused. This is subnormal. People shuffle along in a form of sub-normal existing — they're just existing.

Chapter 2

Useful and non-useful discussion; On evoking relevant information as opposed to non-relevant by limiting oneself to usable and useful knowledge; Avoiding accumulation and intellectualization; The autonomic system of energy management; On aiming oneself upwards and continuously upgrading techniques.

What I wanted to say bears on what you call the application of technique or the application of theory. One can and does learn a certain amount of techniques, terms of reference, ideas and theories; and people very often go about quoting things or bringing them up, saying "Ah, that applies to this" or "this applies to that" or "so-and-so said" or something like that.

What is called recall, or remembering certain phrases or terms of reference – this is useful providing that one brings them up at the right time: referring to something, or stimulated, brought up from the subconscious, or from the memory, or from the unconscious as a result of there being a thought or an action which relates to them. Therefore one is bringing them up as part of a correct memory or thought-process, and not just simply a sort of reactive, regurgitative process. That is one aspect which is important, i.e., bringing up particular things from the memory: aspects, thoughts, quotations from within the Tradition.

The second aspect is of course putting these ideas or thoughts into practice. They shouldn't become merely a source of academic debate or discussion, going on ad infinitum with two or four or however many people involved, discussing the finer points and putting a sort of polish on them; because this can very easily degenerate into the intellectualization of these things: a sort of classification, sorting-out, docketing, labelling, pigeon-holing and amassing of miscellaneous information. It may be very valuable but it must be used in a practical context.

If one talks about self-examination in the sense of looking at oneself, understanding how one reacts to certain situations, how thought-processes or impacts can be stimulated by various extraneous impacts, or by the thoughts or feelings within oneself; one learns about oneself, how one reacts, and how one's thought-processes can be stimulated by injecting valuable trace elements into them.

When they become merely identified as being useful stimuli and are put in a file marked "useful stimuli" and filed away, and the person goes out and tries and finds more useful stimuli which he will then file and build up his filing system or memory banks full of these useful stimuli — when is he going to use them? When is he or she going to put them into practice? "Oh I'm waiting for the right moment," "Oh I'm waiting for the right combination of circumstances."

A person may imagine a Utopian combination of circumstances — plenty of time, comfort, no problems, no disturbance, nothing — "and then I will think about x, y or z." This is perfectly reasonable and perfectly human to have this attitude, but it is imposing a limitation on the useful stimulus. You've got it ready and you're going to trot it out when the circumstances, according to your evaluation, are propitious — right. Now they might never be propitious, according to the list you have prepared of what are propitious circumstances. There might be one element missing and you say, "Well, everything is not quite right, therefore we'll wait for that." Meanwhile one is filling the files up and it becomes a race of trying to put together those stimuli with propitious circumstances. So you're looking for more and more specific propitious circumstances, and you've got a backlog of useful impacts; you're trying to put the two together, right? If these propitious circumstances don't come, one tries to provoke them: "I'm going to leave my job, sell everything and go and sit on a mountain, and just think about these things." Right. Apart from the fact that it is certainly by no means always necessary to sell up everything and go and sit on a mountain — if you do such a thing I guarantee that you will be more confused than if you tried to handle them within the context of your study or work or whatever; because it can be a Pandora's Box.

There you are; you've left your job, your responsibilities, sold everything up and sitting in a mud hut or whatever, and you say, "Right, this is now a propitious circumstance; I will now look at everything." So you open the box and there is a whole stack of these stimuli which then descend on you and drive you nutty—because you're trying to handle them all at the same time. You've opened the box, they've all come out and you'll be knee-deep in them and you aren't able to handle them.

So what do you do? *What you do is: you handle them as they come along within the context of the situation in which you find yourself.* This is in the world and not of the world. Don't try and dictate in advance "I will only look at this or that or that, given that this, that and the other circumstance apply in the other case," because if you don't put the act together you get more tense, more confused.

You certainly take note of the useful impacts and useful positive tactics, techniques, advice, whatever, and you remember them and you put them out; you use them in almost no matter what circumstance. Sometimes they will take, sometimes they won't take; but don't try and dictate to what degree they will take or be successful. *Certainly, aim for them to be as successful as possible,* but don't then say "It didn't come up to my expectations." How are you going to measure it?

You can imagine what you expect, but what you actually get is not always the same thing. This can lead to disillusionment, confusion, dissatisfaction, unhappiness and so forth. *Rely more on the actual, not automatic, but autonomic system which takes this energy on; and uses it, releases it, enhances perception, enhances situations autonomically— that is, it relates to a circumstance and is in a way drawn out by the character of the circumstance.*

It feeds into the system imperceptibly and is used by the system; sometimes perceptibly, sometimes imperceptibly. To impose any form of measurement on it can be either to enhance it by imagination or to limit its influence. "When I read this or when I do that my nose will become big and red and flash."

If you have decided that, and the effect of that actual impact is that your nose will become big, red and flash and also that your ears will wag simultaneously—you're preventing your ears from wagging simultaneously by limiting its impact to only your nose flashing. So don't say "My nose will flash, my ears will wag, and my toes will flicker at the same time," because you're imagining, you're spreading it too thinly. The other way, if you say "No, only my nose will flash," you're also imposing a limitation on it. So don't overstretch it, don't underplay it.

Allow the result of the impact to come out and relate to a similar circumstance. *Like attracts like.* In circumstances where there is something of a positive nature present – if it is related to something positive within oneself, this contact will be maintained.

The form of contact – whichever way one considers it – must always be on a higher level, i.e., upwards. Slightly upwards. Because the attempt and the direction on an activity, on whichever level it is, should always be pointed. *One should always aim, whichever activity one is doing – in life, in the Tradition, in everything – in an upwards way. Because by definition, the upward trajectory is more positive than a horizontal one, because that inevitably has a decay factor in it; and certainly not a downwards one, because that by definition must be a negative curve. But if one is aiming reasonable higher, the decay factor can be of small magnitude.*

One should strain oneself, stretch oneself, within limits – not overstretch, because that leads to tension, to confusion, to problems, to dissatisfaction with one's own performance and so on. One should then assimilate, feed in, gather, and use – otherwise these are all theory and are interesting as terms of reference, they are interesting reasons for interminable discussion. They shouldn't be allowed to become interminable discussion; *they're too valuable to become intellectual chewing-gum.*

All techniques are updated by the capacity of the person. You might say, "Oh I've used that, so that is now finished, I don't use that any more" – no. Take a technique which one uses at a very low level – as a person develops, so he develops the capacity to use a similar technique in a more refined way. If you learn how to learn, you can learn the A B C of a foreign language. Now the same technique that you use to learn the A B C – once you've mastered that, you upgrade it to the point where you can then write the language. And then you upgrade the same technique and you can compose poetry in that language. It's the same technique: you're not discarding the learning cells which you've used just to learn the A B C, no you're upgrading them to meet the challenge of your upgraded knowledge – but unless these tactics and these techniques are used, and the correct compatible techniques are used in compatible circumstances, you can go on attempting to apply these techniques and saying: "Well, I'm applying them and they don't work."

It's a choice of tactic or technique which is important, which you feel. You may call it reasoning it out, or going through a few of them in the mind and producing one; whichever tactic you use is valid as long as the measurement is based on your feeling within the Tradition.

There is always a danger that it will be a conditioned choice, and one has enough conditioning going about to allow the tactics or the techniques of the Tradition to fall into the area of conditioned reflex type of thing. So briefly, learn the techniques; don't just stack away a lot of terms of reference.

Terms of reference by definition are used for reference leading to the application of the knowledge you get by referring to the terms of reference. A telephone book could be considered a reference book. You look at it when you want a telephone number: you then use the telephone to communicate, to make a call, to do business or whatever you're doing. You don't just say "Ah yes, that is the telephone number, fine." Big deal. You don't consult the telephone book all the time, you consult it when you need it and then you use the piece of information through a technique, which is dialing or pressing buttons or whatever, to achieve your aim, which is communication.

So don't just amass. Don't discuss—don't thrash out the finer points of it: polishing, polishing, polishing, polishing a thing. *Polishing, polishing, polishing, polishing yourself, yes—that is the idea. But polishing, polishing, polishing, polishing the technique, no. The technique is sufficiently polished: apply it.*

Chapter 3

INTENTION AND GRATITUDE

On separating both from superstition; Preventing gratitude from becoming a formalized and automatic reaction by seeing how it works; The importance of basic intent and how to develop it.

There are a couple of areas of activity or behaviour within the context of the Tradition which are functional, positive, important and consciously practised, and are consciously to be seen to be present and to be practised. These factors are intention and the other one is gratitude.

In the Tradition and in reading about aspects of the Tradition, one will see both these factors quite clearly laid out. Yet over the centuries, because of interpolation or interpretation or commentary or misunderstanding, they have been covered over by superstition, magic, or various factors which have taken them a little bit out of the positive area and brought them into sort of folklore, and given them a sort of wishy-washy character. *There's nothing at all wishy-washy about intention or gratitude.*

Let me take gratitude first. Gratitude is one very positive factor which has gone very much into an area of superstition. Superstition in the sense of maybe something comes together or something works or something good happens or something fortunate happens and, furtively — sometimes quite naturally but sometimes furtively — people cross themselves, touch wood, mutter "thank goodness" or something like that; and feel a little bit as if they should be grateful but they don't know to what degree, or whether it's merely averting bad luck, if they are grateful or not. And this becomes very wishy-washy and imprecise.

The idea of gratitude is a very positive and a very clear one. Somebody, some idiotic fellow, once said that "Man should not live on his knees except in gratitude." This is a very imprecise and ill-thought phrase, because it implies that at any time that the person feels gratitude, for whatever situation, that they should automatically fall on their knees. This is very often inconvenient, it's unnecessary and it becomes a sort of gut reaction.

Normally one feels gratitude for something which has gone right, gone correctly — something which other people call "a stroke of luck," a coincidence, something fortunate, or "it was my lucky day" or this, that and the other thing. Well, all these are possibilities, but they are inexact. They are just as inexact as "we Scorpios are like that;" "we Aquarians are like this;" "I am French;" "he is Chinese." These are sort of geographical or other labels which people place on themselves, and they excuse things, "Oh yes, it happened because today is Friday and Jupiter is in my ascendant and therefore it'll work out." Well why doesn't it work out every Friday?

So what has that got to do with gratitude? Gratitude does not need to back a person superstitiously every time anything which they have set out to do, or as a result of a culmination of their activities or efforts, or a coordinated effort among Friends and others, comes to a positive culmination — that they should feel some extraordinary amazement. They can have a feeling of wonder, they can wonder how it worked, why should it work, did it work, has it worked — but they should basically have a feeling of gratitude for having had assistance or aid or direction; or a mixture of having aid, assistance, direction — and having put the thing together themselves. They should feel gratitude towards themselves in the sense they should feel gratitude for the fact that they have had the common sense, terms of reference or experience, to be able to put things together.

Should one then express a gratitude constantly, to what degree, how much, and in what form? And the answer is: in many forms, in all forms, under varying circumstances. People say for instance: "There but for the grace of God," or in some places people see a priest and they cross themselves. I know how they feel, but this is a reaction to some sort of superstitious situation. A black cat crosses your path — in some parts of the world a white cat is supposed to be unlucky. They're both unlucky; if you are looking upwards, you will fall over them. It doesn't make any difference to a colour: if you believe that a black cat or a white cat will bring you good luck or bad luck, you can attract it. Like attracts like. Before you're going to do something, you don't have to rush out and find a white cat or a black cat and carry it into the interview with you or whatever. It's like the man who, on seeing a notice on top of the moving staircase "dogs will be carried," rushed out, found a dog, carried it down in order to get on the train. This is a misconception of a situation. For instance one sees some unfortunate person, a cripple or somebody in unfortunate circumstances — one doesn't immediately rush into the nearest place of worship and indulge in great ramblings or great protestations of gratitude. No, one records the fact that one is grateful, that one is not in that unfortunate situation, to a certain extent. As a matter of course one is recording it, one is noticing it, and one is using it as a term of reference.

There is a difference between having a positive and useful attitude toward these things and getting rid of the superstitions, which are imprecise. They will let you down at the wrong moment, which is the moment you need them most. You can festoon yourself with tasbees*, crucifixes, stars of David, crescent and star, whatever you like — this won't protect you from your own stupidity.

Gratitude is a recognition of the fact that, by thought, actions, feelings, by being in contact, by tuning in, one has been pushed towards, pulled towards, forced towards or whatever, combinations of circumstances which are useful and proper. One is grateful for the fact that these circumstances and sets of circumstances are the stepping-stones to other circumstances, to other things, to other developments within oneself in the world, or in other circumstances which one might call unworldly. Right. So that one strikes a harmony between.

This brings one to, again, the idea of the intent. *When one's intent, before one does something, or at almost any time — one's intent should be to be positive, to be balanced, to look at oneself, at situations, at oneself in regard to situations — and make a harmonious intention toward that situation or towards that person.*

The basis of a positive situation is a positive intent. If one's intention is fraudulent, dishonest, based on laziness; these by definition cannot produce a positive result. If one's intention is less correct, less positive, it can get beefed up by time, by harmonizing oneself with the situation; it can be improved and positive can result. But it is a far greater battle than to start off with certain positive intentions and terms of reference.

* Prayer beads

People know themselves what their intent is. The people who get into problems with themselves and with other people are the ones who try to be clever with themselves in the sense that they generally have an intention in a situation, and they perhaps try to hide that intent. They may be able to hide that intent from other people but they can't hide it from themselves. This of course precipitates a battle within themselves, because it's quite obvious that if one part of the consciousness has a particular intent and is trying to convince the other part that this intent is really something else, obviously the other part is going to revolt and is going to say "Rubbish! This is a product or a figment of part of me." So you might try and explain to somebody else, "My intention is this, that and the other thing" – they have no way of knowing. "But I happen to know because I'm part of you, so don't try and sell me that thing: 'I am collecting for Father Christmas' when you are really collecting to buy yourself a bicycle." Because this provokes tension within oneself.

People say "the negative in me, the positive in me" – and they juggle these terms around. With a situation where a malicious or dishonest or lazy or stupid intent is being pushed by the negative onto the positive – of course there is friction. One is catering for the positive; one is boosting up the positive, and of course there is friction. And this friction either destroys the situation, or gets the person uptight and nervous, or makes them fight with other people, or makes them edgy, or makes them basically dissatisfied with themselves, or other people, or the circumstances, or all of these things.

I'm not saying that one should always, in every action at all times, aim for an absolutely saintly intent: this would be very utopian, very nice, but unless one uses the external defences which are necessary within the world, you get torn to pieces within twenty-four hours by everybody.

One's intent within is something which one shares with oneself and which one develops and which one is using. This is not to be mixed up with the external. Somebody comes up and demands my wallet and I say a prayer for him and I hand my wallet over. No. You either call a policeman, hit him, run away, or do something: you certainly don't say a prayer for him. You can strike him to the ground and then say a prayer *over* him, that's different. But don't mix: people are constant mixers. "Better to say a prayer or to get the train?" Well, if you're going to lose your job if you don't get the train, then there is no question. "I will get my reward in heaven" — yes, but you need your pay packet at the end of the week.

The mixture of things: "Is it better to sell fish or to sell *kilims*?" These questions are certainly imprecise — they're based on a sort of raring intent. "What do I want to do? Do I want to get attention or do I want to sell fish? Or do I want to sell *kilims*? Or do I want to make an impression on my teacher — 'Oh what a good fellow, selling *kilims*' — because he doesn't like fish?"

A person can afford to indulge their hidden and open prejudices, or likes and dislikes — provided they are not intrusive upon other people. They can be a source of astonishment and very often are, but if they are merely for astonishment or even hilarity, this is fine because there's nothing wrong with hilarity. People breathe deeply when they laugh so it's always good. But when it becomes intrusive upon other people's privacy or anything, then a limit has been reached.

If one is conscious of this, then one doesn't go beyond limits; because if one's intention in starting and doing something is a blend of consideration for other people — normal politeness, friendship and so forth — then this intent prevents one from becoming either obnoxious or embarrassing or a burden on other people. If, as a result of unfortunate circumstances, one's intent becomes diluted, and the amount of energy available or impetus in a particular circumstance becomes less; this can be an excuse for lack of carry-through. But there is always a backup to the intent; there are many — I don't need to name them because you can find them and know them — there are many tactics and formulations to get energy in certain given situations when one feels the need for backup.

The backup is there; the reservations people have — "Do I have the right to ask for it?" "How do I use it?" "How do I know that it's not overkill?" "Shall I get enough?" — these don't really have to perturb one. Because in no way is one going to get more energy than one can use, or less energy than is necessary. It may not be the amount of energy that you think is necessary, because unfortunately people's judgement is befogged and befouled by various factors, so that they can't basically be trusted to indent for x thousand million ergs of energy or whatever. Because they're either underkill or overkill, and then if they think that they have some left over, they won't know whether to post it back to somebody, or to keep it, or put it in the fridge or what, and then they get added confusion, and who needs more confusion?

If the intent is equilibriated and balanced from the beginning, there are built-in safeguards. If the intent is correct, then the situation will develop. It may not develop in the way one imagines it, or in the same time-scale or area, but it will develop. When it culminates in a correct situation, a positive useful situation for the person themselves, for the people with whom they're associated, or for somebody completely for the moment unassociated; then they can feel quiet satisfaction — some people call it *kaif* — you can take a step forward and call it "orgueil" — or you can also have a feeling of gratitude. One has learnt a lesson, one has used terms of reference, tactics, or energy correctly, and — thank whatever — it has worked. That is not a superstitious thing. One will then rush to St. Neanderthal's shrine and light three candles — this is per- fectly good, I'm not knocking it, I'm not saying "don't do that," but I'm saying put your gratitude down to a particular use of a useful and posi- tive energy. There is no religious, geographical, racial, political, social or other monopoly: "St. Ignatius is better than St. Neanderthal because he was canonized before; therefore bah!" This becomes then a social thing and the pecking order and hierarchical thing.

Basically, two things: *the intent is fueled by the energy, and the cul- mination of that produces the gratitude and quiet contentment which comes together with it. It's not a stop-start; the situation produces the capacity to appreciate the culmination, and hence the gratitude is propor- tionate to the amount of satisfaction.*

Now proportions vary. That doesn't mean to say that you manage to find a golden disc of Bob Dylan and you go raving mad immediate- ly as a result. One can go home and listen to it and have enormous satis- faction which one can demonstrate by the satisfaction of achievement to oneself — the way you demonstrate it is different for everybody. Some people may go hooting and snarling and growling and yelling and bang- ing drums in a situation where somebody else will feel very happy and do nothing in particular. This is the difference between the exterioriz- ing of the feeling or not — it depends also on personality, circumstance, and so on; there's no rigid way. You know, most of the world look at the English and say "Good heavens, if I were in his position I would be singing and dancing in the street!" And the Englishman is saying: "That was jolly good." This is a different temperament. Neither person has the monopoly of feeling; that everybody should just say "jolly good" or that everybody should go down and sing in the street. Brazilians dance in the street anyway, all the time, whether they have anything to celebrate or not. And by their terms of reference this is perfectly laudable and reasonable, and so it is. So the degree of recognition or gratitude which one feels is proportionate to the person and the circumstance.

Q: To where does one direct gratitude? What does one say?

A: I don't think there is a problem here, because the fact that one is feeling that a thing has happened, that a circumstance has occurred or, whatever the reason for it, and the fact that this factor exists, is a positive factor. So since positive always joins positive, whether one says "Thank God" or "Alhamdullilah" or "Thanks to Mushkil Gusha" or whatever, this is not important in the sense one doesn't have to find out "Whodunnit."

The fact is that one has achieved it, that one has used energy, tactics, technique — one has put the thing together and it has worked. So it is certainly better to tend to direct such thanks or gratitude more specifically, rather than, for instance, to divide it among all the saints in the calendar, as some people do. One then spends all one's time lighting candles and so forth, which is a very admirable thing, but it is spread out a bit thinly. Even that isn't a waste — because the amount of gratitude spread out over that, which is a positive entity, is then scooped up and put together again. But it is much easier if it is actually there rather than being scooped up.

Also, another exactly similar thing is the retrospective. In such-and-such a circumstance, a long way back, a particular thing happened and I'm grateful for that thing having happened. That is an affirmation of one's feeling of positive gratitude. At that point one is cutting away all this "It was because I was carrying a rabbit's foot and a four-leaf clover and I didn't see any black cats and it was a crescent moon and I was standing at the shrine of St. Neanderthal at the same time" — because if you get into that imprecise reasoning; unless you recreate or re-enact those factual circumstances — i.e., the four-leaf clover, rabbit's foot, the piece of the Holy Cross, the goodness-knows-what and the this-that-and-the-other-thing—which is impossible, because the time factor has changed by a minute, by a second, by a millisecond, by a billisecond, by a year.

"Yeah, well it worked last time." Yes, but that was way back, so it won't work again. It might, given the same time configuration, quality, that is the imponderable. "I'll put it off until I can see the moon in the same position in the chink of the glass"—"I didn't see it last night"— yes, because there's a car parked out there. Whose fault is that? The moon? Yours? The car? Then you get into the realm of the two hands clapping in an empty room, do they make any noise? Well the room isn't empty if there are two hands clapping. So that, I mean, answers itself.

So those two factors are very simple. They shouldn't preoccupy one in the sense of over-occupy. They should be present, and they should be capable of being brought up, reminded to remind oneself, and used.

Chapter 4

ON GROUPS AND THEIR FUNCTION

Levels of grouping; Degree of commonality; Basic aims; Filtering out anomalies; The three entities of the group individual as viewed by the Tradition; Individual and group energy; Breaking down conditioned barriers; Establishing shared attitudes to save time and effort; Focusing on common concerns; Replenishing the energy-pool; Role of personality.

Let me talk about the function and the functioning of a Group; functions within a Group are, and should be, on several levels. The basic level is the one in which the individuals agree that they share certain common aims. Their particular or specific motivations vis-à-vis any of these aims may vary. The speed at which they hope to attain them may vary, and also the various other areas of relationship which vary in intensity, in coherence, and melody or harmony. One does not aim to produce a group, which by definition is a number of individuals, all having exactly similar points of view, attitudes, to the same degrees of intensity, or with exactly the same list of priorities.

One can produce this by a system which one uses in musical reproduction, by a series of what are technically called "notch filters" — that is, you take off the top notes or you deepen the bass notes and you jiggle about with knobs and you produce a sort of maximum or minimum permissible. This is possible, and in some areas the person who is teaching reserves the right to do this, but it is not an imposition of what is called a norm: "Thou shalt react like this" — "Thou shalt think like this" — "Thou shalt have this amount of momentum or impulse" or something like that, because although it's a group, one is looking at people and dealing with people as individuals composing a group. Supposing you say "Okay, if it's a number of individuals that can be in a group, why a group and why not just a number of individuals living here, there, everywhere and so forth?" The reason is that an individual in the group, from the point of view of the Tradition, has three fairly distinct entities.

One of these is as themselves — the other is as a member of a group, and the third is as a person within the Tradition. So you might say that they wear three hats.

None of these relationships are in competition with each other, nor should they be nor are they on any sort of collision course with each other. They don't compromise each other, they act in a harmonious way. A person who is teaching will relate to each individual person in a group as an individual; also as a member of the group; also in terms of the teacher's overall function within the Tradition in relation to that individual as a person in the Tradition. Each of those three entities is treated, stimulated, damped down, x, or y, or whatever, according to either the situation, or their state, or the needs of the circumstance — and inevitably, the aim is to produce a harmonious situation between these three entities.

The old story: "Which one of me is drinking this tonic?" There should not be, really, a situation where a person has to ask this question. Certainly not constantly, because all these shade into each other, they're not distinct entities. They boost each up and they help each other — any other situation: "Which of me?" — "Am I an individual, am I a member of the Group, am I in the Tradition?" — causes confusion or can cause confusion: "How should I react to a specific situation?" "Which card shall I play, this one or that one?" It should become, not an automatic, but an instinctive tuning-in. "Which aspect am I using at this particular moment?" — not, again, the constant examination: "Is it this one; shall I try that? How about this? Oh, I don't know" and so forth — who needs any more confusion?

You have the three entities which are harmonious to each other. And contact, information, exercises and activities feed, nourish, stimulate, damp down, each one of these three — according to the state of the person at the time, which is ever-changing — again, within a reasonable harmonious context. *Why the need for a group at all? Because in a situation where there is a group, the group as a group produces a certain type of energy. In a situation where a person may be doing an exercise or reading something or thinking about something within the context of the Tradition in a positive way, they are producing a certain amount of positive and useful energy. As a participant in a group, doing a similar thing, or listening to something, they are producing their individual energy and they're also producing a group energy. As an individual they produce energy which they are capable of using. Within the group, they produce energy which they are capable of using as individuals, and which the group as a group is capable of using. The important distinction is that, in a group context, there is a pool of energy which is produced—what I would call "group energy"—right. The group benefits from that energy, from the transmission, exchange, interchange, of this energy—and an individual in the group can benefit according to his or her need.*

The amount of energy which is produced by a group activity—is in a sort of pool—if you have ten people in a group the amount of energy is not divided into ten and dispersed, distributed among the people. It can be that one person can't use the particular energy which is available at that time, whereas another person or two people or three people out of that ten might have a considerable need for that particular type of energy in a particular given moment—in which case, the whole amount of pooled energy will go to that person or persons who need it most, or who can use it best.

As I've said before, a person does not know how much energy they are producing. A group doesn't know how much. There is no system of measurement which they can apply. They can say, and I hope they do, that that was a good and productive meeting and I felt good and one or two things were clarified, or whatever: or it was terrible, or I didn't feel right or something like that—but they don't actually know, so therefore they can't go in saying "Well, I want to get a hefty chunk of energy tonight" or "Oh I don't think I need it" or "I'll just have a nibble and see" or something. No, because this would be a conditioned and demanding attitude.

If they need it and if it's present, they can take of it. Again it's not the question "Oh, do I have the right to?" Not only does the person have the right to it, they have an obligation to themselves to make use of it.

It's no big deal to say, "Oh dear, I am so humble and insignificant" and so forth, or "I don't have the right to" because that is underplaying it—neither should they be greedy. Since they have no control over the amount they take, there is no fasting and there is no greed. They can also take a certain amount of good energy, consistent with the amount of energy that they themselves can usefully use, and take it with them, and use it in a future circumstance: an hour later, a day later, a week later or whenever.

Again, this energy is not a perceptible thing which they carry away and suddenly, next week they get in a traffic jam, so they dole it out to the exasperated drivers and everybody feels marvelous — no. They don't because apart from the fact that they could conceivably make a mistake, they would also, having been told that "Right, take this and use it usefully," they would either look around desperately for opportunities to use it, or they would keep it in case they used it wrongly, and probably not use it. So therefore they are merely — it's more than merely, actually, but anyway — *they are carriers of this energy, and if and when and as they come in contact with a situation where they can usefully transmit it and disperse it, then this takes place.*

So, you have a group situation. It's a reasonable, normal situation; it has other, reasonably useful sort of spin-offs. If one has a number of people working together with certain specific aims in view, for certain specific interests, who read similar books, have established and developed certain terms of reference — many things happen as a result. Firstly, certain conditioned barriers are broken down — conditioned barriers in the sense that one will find that it is much easier to discuss certain things which perhaps may be impalpable, slightly vague or imprecise areas of what before one might have considered somewhat funny or weird or superstitious, if one is a bit shy of talking about it — that sort of thing.

One finds that one can discuss it with people without necessarily using commonly-shared terms of reference immediately. I mean you say to somebody "I read such-and-such a thing" or "I listened to such-and-such a thing" or "I visited such-and-such a place and I felt something or I don't know what" — now if you were talking to somebody who possibly has had a similar experience, you have established a harmony with that person. You have established a term of reference in this particular area without it being a specified term of reference.

What I am saying is that you don't have to get down to the "Oh, that was number 3 syndrome on the left" before everybody agrees to it. You don't have to spell things out quite to the degree at which you have to then search for — "You know, it was ..." — "I felt hot, cold, sad, tired, hungry, sick" or what. One defines the term of reference by harmonizing with another person or other people, and you get into the area of not having to define it, which a. saves a lot of time, and b. this is a horribly overplayed word, but still — there is a shared attitude to certain things and certain places, and you don't have to go through re-explanations of certain things.

If you use a certain phrase or a certain technical term, or you say "relaxation" or "exercise" or something like that — you don't have to then add in parentheses: "that is to say so-and-so." One establishes certain common denominators, and therefore, you establish a certain common language. This makes for a lesser degree of tension. That is not to say that when I say that certain barriers come down, I don't mean that everybody paints themselves blue and dances round Hampstead Heath or something like that, because this would be unnecessarily extreme and cold and everything else — neither do the normal barriers of politeness and consideration and so forth go down. In fact they increase — as the responsibility and feeling towards other people increases, so does the consideration and so forth increase.

It means that, if you like, the sort of hedging about, parrying, or over-tenseness, or any form of intense seeking to establish terms of reference — doesn't play any sort of necessary part. It is establishing a harmonious communication with other people and finding that one can gradually discuss aspects of one's thinking with other people in an effort, not to convince or convert somebody else, but very often to clarify one's own thinking by seeking an objective, detached judgment about a certain aspect of one's thinking which one hasn't yet been able to achieve on one's own.

You might say, "Well, one does that all the time." You want to buy a car so you ask three or four people "What do you think of such-and-such a car?" and "What is it like on petrol?" and "Is it comfortable?" and "What is the heater like?" etc. Yes, that's okay, and that's a perfectly reasonable thing to do. You go to a local pub and see a number of worthies and say to them, "I hear old George is selling a horse, what do you think?" And they'll say, "Oh, well, no, I don't know"... or something — that's a perfectly reasonable topic of conversation.

If you go into the same place, and there are a bunch of worthies, and you say to them: "You know, life is this, that and the other thing" they'll say "Oh, Landlord, give him a double brandy and he'll forget about it" or something like that — because people normally don't really want to know. If somebody says to you, "How are you?" and you say, "Well, as a matter of fact, now that you ask I am getting ..." Owww, good grief, and they never ask you again, because they don't want to be told "My knee hurts and my arches have fallen and I have a toothache." It's a convention. People isolate themselves from each other — as a form of protection, this is necessary and it is, under certain circumstances, perfectly laudable.

But it is necessary also for a person to have the opportunity — short of the hundred dollars an hour for the psychiatrist's couch — to be able to converse about various, what one might call for want of a better word, esoterica, and all that that implies — without as I say propounding these questions: you know, "I was sitting in the barn the other day thinking what is the meaning of life ..." and people will say, "Well, I don't know, but as far as I'm concerned, I think the end of the world is nigh because Oxford won the Varsity match, and ended Cambridge's five-year run ..."

Well that is the conditioned reaction: if one asks a question like that of a worthy in a pub, one deserves whatever reply one gets. And if you therefore go out and consider that as a result of that, the end of the world is nigh, that is the level of your satisfaction.

However, if you're in a position where you can discuss in a fairly reasonable way — I'm not talking about this sort of "We're all in this together, let's all bare our souls" and all that sort of thing, because this has gone on ad nauseam for generations and it doesn't always produce a very useful circumstance. One can discuss, compare notes about certain things. When I go out of the room you can always sit down and discuss what I've said, and some people will say, "This is a load of rubbish!" — but if a group of people are discussing something, or comparing notes within a group context, it should be on a matter which concerns all of them to a similar degree.

That is to say, it should preferably — not always — because in the Tradition we don't limit discussion to a specific thing — but it should preferably be something which is of recent moment, or of recent origin or a recent thing; so that any contribution or analysis or idea about it can be more or less fresh in people's minds. It can be, for instance, that a group meets and, say, listens to a tape or something and then talks about it afterwards. I'm not inviting a series of penetrating analyses on what I have said: "What do you think about it?" because that's always a bit of a leading type of question, and as yet there is an understandable degree of reticence — polite or idiotic or whatever, it doesn't make any difference. The person may say, "Well I don't particularly want to give an in-depth analysis" — neither are they in fact required to. "It's now your turn to tell me what that was."

Certainly, if one wants to give an opinion as to how tension or something affects one, that's perfectly all right. Again, this is not the opportunity of taking everybody through a sort of step-by-step blow-by-blow history of one's life, and everybody's eagerly waiting for their turn next — because then you have the sort of pent-up thing.

Any group situation should be a harmonious interchange of energy, and a consciousness of the sharing and the useful using of this energy. Not just expounding for expounding's sake, but an exchange of attitudes rather than opinion, because opinion can be very much a result of all sorts of present physical, psychological, social, economic and other circumstances, which apply at a given moment. So a person's opinion is likely to be coloured by the circumstances in which they're living. A person's opinion is therefore more often than not a sort of reactive thing. A person's attitude, to the degree that they like to explain it, is more likely to be useful to other people, because they may think, "Aha, well, that is my attitude" or "That was my attitude" or "Should that be my attitude?" or "That is another attitude to take up."

So harmonious interchange of energy is a function of a group, and the group energy has a very distinct and useful function, because it replenishes the reservoir of energy every time it meets. Equally, when the individual person is absent from the group, or in a circumstance when they're not physically present, if their function in that particular circumstance is useful to the group, the energy which they may have produced will go into that group-pool of energy, although they're not physically present in the group at the time. So they're functioning, you see, on the three levels.

Groups are not established in the sense that one just goes out and takes the first eight people in a bus queue and makes them into a group. This can be done – one does it in the army. You take a hundred goons and blast them for three months, and make them into a company. Their function is to function as an army company, that's all. If they don't, they'll be killed, either by their officers or the enemy or by both, therefore they have one function, one solid function, one inflexible function and they do it.

In establishing a Group in the Tradition one aims to establish a basic harmony, a basic sharing experience, a basic capacity of transmission and reception. It is not a loss or diminishing of this famous personality which everybody talks about all the time, because, again within the context of the Tradition, the personality – whatever that means – is not really very important. It is not a sinking of one's identity in a sea of whatever – no. It is an active, positive participation in an agreed activity to the benefit of the individuals as individuals, and as members of the group.

One aims, on as many levels as possible, not only just to harmonise, because that's just the basis – but to increase the harmony. Again, it doesn't mean everybody living in everybody else's pockets and all that sort of thing. There are very many ways of increasing the harmony of relationships, very often not very staggering ones. "Oh let's all go over and do so-and-so's washing" or paint the house or something like that. This may be all very well, and it's a useful, human and decent and social sort of thing – but again, one doesn't always have to go for the perceptible grand-slam big things.

If one is conscious of one's membership of a group, by very simple things – if one thinks kindly of a person and wishes them well – this is an automatic amount of positive energy which one is sending to that person. Everything which is based upon a positive intention, however fleeting – it may be several seconds – has positive impact. It goes into a positive pool. So any degree of useful, harmonious relationship benefits the group and the individuals. And it is after all groups forming together which make up the Tradition.

The Tradition works through people. The Tradition does not exist in order to show people how clever it is. Those of us who teach know very well how clever the other ones who teach you are. That means we don't have to sit together and have mutual admiration societies. We agree that we're all brilliant and marvelous and everything like that and we go out and do our work.

So unless the Tradition, the function of which is to teach and lead and guide and push, functions through people—unless these people develop the harmonious capacity to benefit from and use the energy, they just go round in circles.

Chapter 5

On using the Tradition as a framework for defining a problem, clarifying its nature and seeing it in proportion, stripping it down to its essentials without exaggerating it, and ultimately solving it.

There is a little difference between the three words: solutions, choices, decisions. They can all apply to—for instance—a problem. Everybody looks for a solution to a problem; everybody looks for a way to resolve a problem and everybody has slightly different techniques in the way they look at a problem or a situation, examine it, and try and find a solution.

Given that a large percentage of problems, confusions or questions are different—that is to say they can be social, health, economic or professional ones—it would not be correct to say that there is a typical way of examining a situation or a problem in order to try and work out a solution or work one's way through it.

Since the nature of the questions or the problems or the confusions vary, so the techniques or the apparatus which you use to find a solution—or explain them to yourself—vary also. So let's have a look at how they vary, why they vary, and how one applies a technique or a series of techniques in order to find a solution to them. Or if the problem is a question, how one tries to find the answer to that question—and is there a technique or a framework of analysis of all sorts of different problems which can be applied, irrespective of the nature of the problem?

That is to say, is there a framework, is there a viewpoint, say, from the point of view of the Tradition? Can one take up a position vis-à-vis different sorts of problems, and, by using an efficient technique, find the answer or solution or something true from the point of view of the Tradition by applying terms of reference and techniques of the Tradition? The answer is yes.

The solution-finding techniques, the problem-identifying-and-solving techniques, the question-looking-at and answer-finding techniques, are all very similar. However, we don't start—and I'm not starting—by saying: "Apply x or y or z technique to a particular thing" for the simple reason that before you start applying a technique to solve a problem, answer a question, solve a doubt or to find one's way through a confusion; you have to have that question, problem, situation or confusion, nicely and clearly delineated and laid out on the table in front of you—then you can start to work on it.

It's no good getting a piece of meat and covering it with all sorts of cloths of different colours, sizes, and shapes, etc., then putting it on the table and applying the cutting technique to it. You can't see it, you don't know where the bone is until you feel it, you don't know which way you're cutting it. So, logically and normally, you don't do that.

If you're sawing a piece of wood, you don't put it behind you and saw it, and hope that "It's wood and I have a saw" so we must cut. It will cut you or the wall, and at best it will be a hit-or-miss and disappointing experience. "I used a saw under the right circumstances and it didn't cut. Hmmmm." It didn't cut because it wasn't placed properly, it wasn't positioned properly, the cutting instrument was not used in its most efficient manner—and with the best intention, the best will in the world, it is used to only ten percent of its efficiency.

Before you try and use any technique to find your way through questions, problems, confusions and so forth, you must as far as possible isolate the specific problem, question, difficulty, confusion to yourself; look at it, and after having looked at it, and as they say, examined all four sides of it, apply one technique or other to it. It sounds simple, so you say "What's the problem?" Now seventy-five percent of the problem is clarifying its nature, getting it on the table, identifying it—and then, whether you use a hammer or a stone or a brick, if its nature is a nut, you can crack it with all these things.

But if it's in a box, you don't know if it's a nut, a piece of iron, or a piece of wood. You hit it with a hammer, you saw it with a saw, and you get a cutting-torch and you cut the box up, and you say "Well, I used all three, it must be one of those three. So one way or another, I cut it." Fine, yes, you may have, but this is a waste of the two other things you're using. If it's metal, you will damage the saw and you will break the hammer.

We come down to the source, really, of the whole question, and that is: what has gone into making this problem into a problem or a question or a confusion? It can be things which are in fact completely irrelevant, but they're so much part of a person's conditioned thinking or reaction, that in fact they don't notice that they are wrapping the meat up in 200 pieces of cloth and putting it into a box and everything like that. They say "Right, I'm going to do that, I'm going to look at this." They've already wrapped it up because "I always do it like this." "We Brazilians are like that." "We Afghans are all mad in any case." "I saw somebody doing it like this." "I heard it on the radio." "I thought it was a good idea." Somebody said: "If I were you, I would do this."

What you are very often doing is looking at the situation, question or problem, through a series of filters, which are the conditioning – social, political, religious, physical, x, y, z, and so on. Some of the filters are coloured, some of them are opaque, and they all prevent you from coming to proper grips with the problem because they prevent you from seeing it clearly – that's all.

When I say that's all, I mean it's a lot, actually, because you've got it out of this miasma of conditioning: "Oh, I could never do that," "Oh, it's too complicated," "Ah well, you see it relates to this, that and the other thing." Once you've made the dissection and got it out and shone a light on it, you're two-thirds of the way home, because you can tackle it with one of several techniques. It has lost its mystery. It's not covered up in a box, you can focus on it, it's there. It's a banana. You say "It's a banana – But it's a banana wrapped in this, covered with that, under the thing it could be dynamite."

But it's a banana. So you say "But that's a banana." I can eat it, cut it up, throw it out of the window, give it to somebody. Yes, but man goes through the most incredibly tortuous, difficult, conditioned suffering and whining before he gets to the point of: "Oh, it's only a banana." Yes, it is only a banana. It was only a banana; that which made you think that it was something extraordinarily complex, menacing, negative in character, was in fact you – your thinking.

If you convince yourself and you are conditioned and brought up by social, national, political, religious or any other conditioning to believe that all bananas are cannibal; then of course you see a banana snarling at you through the bars and naturally your reaction is one of fear and "Ah, that savage banana." "Aha, as long as it's in a cage with the bars between me and the banana — fine." Now you can say: "Who's afraid of a banana?" I'll tell you who's afraid of a banana. Everybody — in a different way.

Not the banana, something else. If you take a banana to somewhere where nobody's ever seen a banana, and you say to them: "Now, this is a banana" — they might very well say "We don't know what that is; it's yellow and it just lies there, it doesn't do anything, it doesn't say anything, but it's hibernating, and at the end of winter, whew ... nobody will be safe within fifty miles!"

You can build upon a race memory, a cult memory, and all that sort of thing ... "The banana that came in from the cold" or something like that ... "It menaced the entire civilization." Hang-ups, cults, reactions can be built and are built successfully on things like that. "I knew a man who was eaten by a banana" and so forth. "I have told my grandchildren, they haven't seen it but they will tell their grandchildren and, oh, all the people I know are afraid of bananas." Ergo, a banana is a savage and desperate and dangerous thing. It's ridiculous. But a banana is what you make it. And cook it, eat it, keep it in a cupboard, throw it at a traffic warden, put it in your petrol tank — it won't necessarily produce an effect. Even if you imagine it will, it won't. It won't replace gasoline or anything like that.

To a large degree, a problem, a question or some confusion, is what you make it. That is cold comfort for somebody who has got problems. "I don't want to make it any bigger than it is, it's trouble enough." Yes, but this is why one distances oneself as much as possible from immediate involvement and has a look at it. Because things flourish and grow, like mushrooms, in the dark — and they agglomerate. That is, "my problems." *Everybody has problems; they all get together.* As I've said again and again, they are problems from the most banal to the most extraordinary — fine. So by identifying them, by isolating them, it doesn't necessarily produce an immediate solution. If it's a problem that you owe somebody fifty thousand dollars; if you have 50,000 dollars — fine. If you haven't, it's still a problem, okay, but at least it's identified as such — it's not "one of my problems." So one has to make a very deliberate and determined effort to get through all these filters which are composed by all sorts of conditioning to get at the problem itself.

I'm not talking about all this garbage of pre-natal influence and all that sort of thing which I really don't care for very much, because there is a point in the examination of a problem, be it a personal one: "My reaction to such-and-such a person or such-and-such a situation is such-and-such." Why? The temptation is to find somebody to blame. Oneself, somebody else, "She always makes me sneeze when I see her." "I fell down a drain once when I saw him, therefore he is responsible for every accident that has happened to me" and the rationalization.

Examination of oneself in a particular situation: "Why did I feel terrible in that particular circumstance?" or "Why did I feel very negative?" or "Why did I go to sleep?" or "Why did I get angry" or "Why was I afraid in that particular context?" Examination up to a useful depth is sufficient. You can go on: Freudian, Jungian, Adlerian, Schopenhauerian, Fischer-Matto-Grosso, Hoffman God-knows-what, pre-natal planetario-Université something-or-other and you confuse yourself, you get lost and somewhere along the way, you most certainly go mad. Because what you need is to find out why that person annoys me, or this person has that effect, or this situation or that ambiance, or why I react to such-and-such a thing like this.

You see, these psychiatrists have a field day—because the great word is "regression" — "get back" to wherever—whereas you want to go only as far back as is necessary for that particular problem. It is not closing your eyes to or avoiding the possible deeper syndromes, capital D capital S, which everybody is crazy about; but this particular motivation reaction syndrome may be, and often is, quite simple.

A person is not encouraged—for the reason that they are considered to exercise intellect—they are not encouraged to say "I hate that fellow because he stinks," or "because he's dirty," or "because he is a plebe." Oh no, it must be something much deeper, significant, and world-shaking; galactically disturbing. People are loathe to diminish. You say to somebody for instance, "You've got a bit of a cold?" "Oh yes, I've got a terrible cold!" Not just a nasty, streamy little cold, no. "I ache in every joint I tell you, I am absolutely dead, finished!" —because it is also a measure of their importance: they don't have a little cold, they have a big cold. They are dying. You don't have a slight draft, you have "drafts everywhere." Nobody likes to admit that there's a draft, it blows on my trousers and therefore I'm uncomfortable. You see, my problem both to myself and to others should be of enormous proportion – it should be important. "Oh, the problems I have!"

It's not, "I owe him fifty francs and I'm going to avoid him in case he asks me" – this is being honest with oneself. You know that you are going to go walking down the street and you're ready to dart into a shop door when you see the person to whom you owe a hundred francs; you start to hate him. Even though he's not out hunting you relentlessly night and day for his hundred francs. He probably would like it back and he would be surprised and gratified if you gave it to him. He's not hunting; but you can make him into the "monster who's destroying my life just for a hundred francs" – okay? And there you go into the basis of neurosis – everything has to be on a sort of histrionic level. It can't be just "I've got a bit of lumbago" – "Oh, my leg, it's about to fall off!" When you exaggerate a problem, a confusion, a difficulty, a reaction, you are exaggerating it because when you're doing it, you know what the reaction will be, what situation you're going to produce by exaggerating this thing.

Obviously you know you're exaggerating, a part of you doesn't like this exaggeration because it's dishonest. If it's a small thing, it's not ghastly, it's not soul-destroying, it's not horribly dishonest or dishonorable – maybe you're telling yourself a white lie. All right, this isn't necessarily terrible, but it can be because that when you start exaggerating the degree of this problem or question or difficulty – because there's a crazy negative part which thrives on this negative exaggeration. The other part of you dislikes this, is disgusted with it and also sees what you're doing.

You know you are digging out a pit for yourself to fall in. This is why you have this degree of revolt: it's not the famous thing which, again, the psychiatrists delight in: "the battle for yourself" – "I'm tearing myself apart!" – this is from hunger. This is garbage. This has no basis of fact at all. It is not possible for a person to say, "I am torn between the positive and negative in me." You know, "Which of me is sitting here?" Me, Ned. Not the 71st me on the left. This is a pure invention. It's an excuse for not grasping the nettle. "It's only the me which sort of passes, ships that pass in the night" – "I'm not a schizophrenic, I'm a multiphrenic, I'm megaphrenic. I didn't really do that, it wasn't the real me."

Well, I can't accept this way of thinking, not because I have such impeccable clarity of thought, but I have too much to do to clutter up my thinking with the indulgences of marginal, inflated, magnified problems, which result from the laziness to apply common sense to identify the thing — and taking out the potion or lotion or technique or whatever, and using it in that situation to solve it.

Everybody's been told for generations, and by me, that people are lazy, greedy, and so forth. Okay. Now it's all right to go about saying, "I am lazy and greedy; I've always thought it and my teacher says so too, ergo, there's nothing I can do about it."

Yes there is. Laziness or greediness is maybe endemic, but it shouldn't become an excuse or a wall or an obstruction against thought and action. As I say, if you make up your mind, "Oh, this is too difficult to understand," "Oh, I could never aspire to that," "Oh, it's impossible for me to understand" — you can end up not even understanding your own language. "Oh me, poor me," and you just make yourself into a sort of hopeless lunatic. Not even lunatic, just hopeless.

So, reverting, and I have said this a million times and I'll probably say it again another million, because it's worth considering. It is worth considering because more and more, the basic techniques, basic knowledges, basic exercises, basic fundamentals of the Tradition need to be learnt, remembered and used — not: "All right, I've learnt those, let's have the next block."

Sure, put those into practice together with other information you're getting, other circumstances, other impulses, other energies, areas, receptivities which you are developing — but hark back to them. You know, "I've passed my driving-test, therefore I'll throw away the highway code" — fine. But the basic techniques, in various permutations — they are applicable if you get the right one.

Remembering is not only remembering. You say you remember yourself, "I remember myself, or I remember when I was young ..." No, remembering is not just self-remembering, but also remembering what you have learnt and putting it into application. Too many people read everything voraciously; you know, "I got through seventy-five books last year, and I can get through another 150 this year and then I'm ready for putting them into action."

Otherwise they become stultified, they're not used if you don't say: "Now how can I apply this one to that situation?" Okay, that is not to say that by remembering them you will automatically make the right choice, but you'll go less off at an angle. You will always be within reaching distance of a technique if you remember. And finally and importantly, remembering deals with remembering when you chose a technique, when you used it, and when it worked, and you remember how it worked and you remember the feeling when it worked. And each time, you try and recapture that time, or that moment or that period, that situation, that ambiance, when the thing clicked and you said: "I did it." It's called quiet satisfaction. All this orgueil business has been developed by our friends across the channel to threaten themselves with and to produce a good income for all the psychiatrists and psychologists. Again, the "orgueil" is what you make it.

There are exaggerations as I said before. If you cook something following a reasonable recipe and it works and it tastes nice — if you run out and you stop everybody who is going past and you telephone everyone you know saying, "I made a steak-and-kidney pie, I tell you, it was great!" this could be considered a certain degree of excessive orgueil. But if you've done it, you have the quiet satisfaction of having done it, you can say, "Aha, see? I did it." The technique was right, the situation was right, I applied it correctly and it worked. It is proof that the technique works and that you can use the technique.

It is, to a degree, child-like — yes, why not? But just as the child gets a simple pleasure out of building a house out of bricks, so — as one progresses in various ways — one gets one's satisfaction out of whatever thing one is doing, whether it be a great intellectual flight of fancy or whether it's constructing a wall or a building or a home for plants. If it's done well you have the right to feel proud, "I did it."

So get the problem out, shake it off from the ones which are adhering to it, look at it, study it, see what technique you can apply — apply it. Don't pussyfoot around, don't wait around, don't lie under the thing with your mouth open waiting for the grape to fall in. Something else might fall in which may not be a grape.

Chapter 6

OBJECTIVE AND/OR SUBJECTIVE REALITY, AND ART

Learning observational skills within the Tradition; Analyzing such observation; Role of reality in observation; How splintering of reality leads to confusion; How mood influences perception; How exaggeration of feelings distorts perception; Avoiding classifications and intellectual pretentiousness; Forefront of memory; How memory establishes its own automatic index; How all positive experience and contact slot in; Oil-spot technique; Role of intention in art and music.

When you are looking at information, and evidence of your own reaction to a person, place or thing; or when you are witnessing somebody else's reaction or behaviour in certain situations, the skill of learning within the context of the Tradition is to observe either yourself or the other people or situation place, and analyse it, as far as you can, correctly.

Analyzing it correctly does not necessarily mean analyzing it according to what you like or what you want to believe or what you want to bring out of a situation. This can be very confusing: a person can do it either unconsciously, because of a lazy pattern of thought — or they can do it because they go into a place, a situation, a relationship with a preconceived idea either of what they are going to see, what influences these things are going to have on them, or what this will provoke in them.

It may be that they decide beforehand what is going to happen; maybe what they want to have happen, or what they think is good for them to have happen. "I should go to such-and-such a place," "I should see such-and-such a thing" and "I should be aghast at its beauty, it's splendour, x, y, z" — so therefore I go and I am dutifully aghast. It proves that I am intelligent or I understand art, furniture, or gardens or whatever thing I am seeing, and therefore I go away patting myself on the back saying "You see, I appreciated it. I understood its magnificence and everything."

Now, observation of people, places, things and circumstances involve a thing which is terribly confusing; I don't know why. You come across this confusion in all areas of western culture, whether it's art, any art form; music, sculpture, painting, anything at all. It's called reality.

People are not content to leave reality as a thing, a context, a term of reference; you have had interminably, since the year dot, definitions: objective reality, subjective reality, and then the plethora of explanations, not of what is subjective reality or what is objective reality, because semantically speaking, subjective reality is what you perceive it to be, or see or think or whatever. And objective reality is, from a detached point of view, what anybody else might see or what it actually is.

Now of course comes the opportunity for every scholar in the world to write books on how you as a person should use both of these realities at the same time, or when to use one, when to use the other, how to juggle them, how to prevent them from obstructing each other or being on a collision course, how they compliment each other, how they supplement your understanding — and they go off into long spiels and great apparent logic, justification, example — and this is all very fulfilling, I suppose. However, as far as we're concerned, there is one reality. There are aspects of that reality: it is not a question of education, intelligence, or anything like that — it is virtually impossible for a person to juggle simultaneously with the so-called objective and subjective realities.

There are, inevitably, contradictions: a person will end up saying "Am I being too subjective?" or "Am I being objective?" This can very easily in very many cases lead to a sort of trauma in which they are developing an almost schizophrenic attitude towards anything: trying to find which is the valid reality which they should apply to this circumstance, place, thing, and so forth. Which of them is subjective, which of them is etc., and you get back into another pattern of thought: "Which of me is smoking a cigarette?" and that sort of thing. And who needs more complex thought which the human being is able to fall into quite easily without any assistance at all?

If one takes up the point of view that reality is reality, there are, we hold, aspects of it. There's no compromise as to what reality is. *Reality doesn't change; it is.* There are many facets of it. What I was saying earlier is an apt example: one might view as absurd a person, a place, a thing, a context, whatever, who would read a book, see something and have a certain reaction – a feedback, an experience, or whatever: physical, emotional, sentimental, intellectual – anything.

Now, what changes? I should interject here that sometimes one will go and experience the same situation at a later time – and things are different. Okay, now one thing is certainly different, and that is that the time element has changed: a person is wiser, happier, sadder, wealthier, poorer, etc.

But another significant factor has changed, and it is perceptible; either the person's perception is different, or quite simply, and it's a basic difference, their mood may be different. Certain situations, certain places, certain experiences, can heighten a state of perception that the person is in at the moment, or it can heighten the mood that they happen to be in at that time. If a person is, and I'm not going to say it's a little-known piece of wisdom, because that sounds ridiculous, but if they are sitting in full summer in the garden of the Generalife*, and they have, for example, a raging toothache; their attitude towards that garden may be somewhat negative, to say the least, because their physical being is very directly involved in experiencing pain, suffering pain, and resisting against pain. In order to prevent them from screaming, jumping in the fountain and bashing somebody or something, they are suppressing certain aspects of themselves, certain reactions. And yet the superconscious or subconscious mind, being what it is, is taking on the effect of the place, and is certainly working.

Subsequent visits to that place after the toothache has gone will either make their full impact, both physically through the five senses, and really blast a person, or their next visit will possibly have some of the associations of pain with it. They may not relate it directly: they might say, "Yes I remember I had a powerful toothache, but I'm better now so I don't think about it" but the memory, the associated factor, is there. So the mood is a factor.

To call it the objective or subjective reality of the garden of the Generalife is, I think, a bit of arrogant nonsense. The Generalife has a reality, a context, an ambience, a place, it's a machine. In that it is working to transmit, broadcast, receive energy – transmit it, influence

* Gardens in the Palace of Alhambra, Granada, Spain

people who visit it — if you try and bring its whole context into conscious mind: "That is the objective and that is the subjective" — you're doing it a disservice, you're trying to dissect it, and you're doing yourself a disservice, you're confusing yourself, in that you're not allowing your perceptions to decide for you — not in terms of which is "objective" and which is "not objective" but which things are positive and beneficial to you in this particular context with which you can relate.

This harks back to a point I made before: if you push it into the realm of these "big" terms: the "objective reality" of the Generalife — "Boing!" like that — you are pushing into the realm of a sort of intellectual exercise, rather than it being an organic relationship. And it's just as simple as that. You con many people who visit some of these places. They say: "I felt something" or "It was tremendous!" "It was fantastic!" or "It was amazing!" or something like that.

If you say to them "Was that experience subjective or objective" — if they say "I looked at the whole place objectively" it means they are possibly students of architecture or gardening or hydraulics or climatology or something like that and they have the capacity to look at it as a carefully constructed garden machine, and be untouched, unmoved by it. If they say "Yes, subjectively speaking, I found it astonishing, powerful, it had something" — they are selling it short. Since there are really no terms of reference which can describe exactly what it's doing, the inference is that it would be influencing them on what is called among the psychologists "the animal level" — as if one were looking at the lawn and thinking "Aaah, I think I'll just crop that grass" or something like that. It's selling the whole context short.

You do not have to go in with two notebooks, one with objective aspects or objective ideas and the other with subjective ideas and note on one and note on the other. If one just allows one's own interior basic sense to tune itself in — without any attempt to push it, because you can't without pushing it away.

You can't reject a positive. You can't always use it to its full, because it depends on capacity and development, but if one does worry about the necessity of having to classify: "Subjectively speaking, I found that rose rather outré" or something — people actually say things like that — I'm constantly amazed when I read things which are what I think are called in press terms "space fillers." Things like reviews of books:

"I read this book and the whole grandiloquent amazingocity of this ver-bosity made me think of some aspects of Sartre's review of Gulbenkian's bank balance" or something, and I am astonished. I must really, in my own horrid way, pay tribute to people who can produce such garbage; I only wish I could get paid for it – I could produce it for days and it would make very entertaining reading, except unfortunately, people might take me seriously and then I'll become a literary guru and that's all I need.

Many avoid the positive or real statements of opinion that Western "intellectual" circles demand that one expound.

And people are supposed to – either in sort of cocktail parties or in conversation or small talk or at vernissages and that sort of thing – to discuss, expound, talk after the theatre and that sort of thing, about "nuances of" you know, Dali's mustache: "I thought that Nabovski in eighteen-o-something had a little more *je-ne-sais-quoi* about it" – I sup-pose it's quite correct, however, as long as it's considered to be exact-ly what it is, that is, normal reasonable small-talk.

I'm not saying, again, that every conversation or thought that one has should be of such an extraordinary profundity that everybody is amazed; either you would sit there for half and hour, thinking it out, and people would say ... like old C. M. Joad. He used to be on the radio, Professor Joad. I remember sitting in my mountain fastness listening to the BBC and whatever they asked him – they would say, "Professor, what do you think about this something?" He would answer, "Well, it depends what you mean by something" – anything, whatever it was at all.

If one is crushed in a bar or something at the opera, and one is asked, "What do you think about so-and-so's costume?" and you think for half an hour – well, firstly the interval's over and everybody's gone back and you're left there thinking it out – or people get fed up and say, "Don't ask him or her a question, because half an hour later you will get some enormous profundity." All they want is small-talk, which is okay, as long as one recognizes what is small-talk and what isn't.

Also, from whom does it come? If you're driving along in caravan with seven or eight cars and there comes a crossroads or something and it's not marked, and you want to go to such-and-such a place; and there are people passing in all directions, inevitably the person in the lead car will ask the way from a person who is manifestly and demonstrably an escaped lunatic — and quite obviously, he will get the sort of direction one would expect from, in this case, an escaped lunatic, which is "There! and twenty miles" so they turn right and go twenty miles, and the road ends in a chasm or something. Everybody's distraught because they haven't applied a single simple thing: that if you're lost in a place you look for somebody who has a certain semblance of being a human being, first — preferably wearing a uniform, policeman, postman, gas man, or somebody who's doing their laundry — somebody who's local. Normal people do it instinctively, people in some caravans don't and they pay the penalty for not doing so.

So it comes down to the point that if, for instance, one is going to an opera, or going to read a book, people are usually brought up or encouraged to read the critics in the Sunday papers about books or theatre or that sort of thing, and many people, understandably, make up their minds on the basis of what the critics say.

So, who do you ask about a particular thing? Well, the answer is somebody who hopefully should know. In a situation, where one wants and one needs a proper explanation, one has to look for a source of that information, and regarding the information or interpretation which one gets — and I have tried this very often with people — you can generally get them to qualify what they say.

For instance, there is a quote which I very often use, much to the distress of my French friends, and that is they preface their words sometimes — but some people, they say "Schopenhauerien parlant" … Or, you get the classic sort of "Well, I mean, Freud said," and then Bla bla bla. If they qualify it, "I don't know, you see, but subjectively, one has the impression that …" — forget it.

Of course if you know the person and respect their point of view, and you consider that their normal amount of intelligence, likes, dislikes and general behaviour is something you can approve of and live with — then certainly. If they say, "Well, this is a subjective opinion but I think such-and-such a play is garbage," or something, then you can go along with it.

If a person says, "Well, objectively speaking …" the tendency is that they are side-stepping it, because you go and see King Lear and somebody asks you, "Well, what was it like?" And you say, "Well, objectively of course, King Lear is very good." Yes, it is—what you're saying is that "I don't wish to commit myself." Very often it's used either as a gambit, to explain their own hangups, i.e., subjective as me: "I think that ..." etc., or objectively: "They say ..." "It would appear that structurally, India is ... whadiyacallit" or whatever.

So the source information, the source of interpretation, or the thing, the ambience, the place, the work of art, piece of music or whatever—is the best source; uncluttered by the so-called twinning or intermingling or whatever they call it of the subjective and—also another catchword which they drop in when they've got you reeling—which is "relatively." Relative to what? I mean "relatively speaking": apart from the fact that, as I say, I am a semanticist and I hate this use of garbage words—which they hardly know the meaning of in any case—but relative to what? "Relatively speaking, a glass of water is a good thing"—ask somebody who is drowning, and see. Relative to his situation it's the most obnoxious thing he can think of, it's all he needs.

Equally, you ask kiddies about making sandcastles, they love it—you ask someone who has crawled ninety-seven miles to an oasis and found it dry what he thinks of sand. So what's this comparison? "I suppose it was relative"—but relative to what? He danced relatively well, but relative to whom? In comparison with ... By comparison to? Now it's not only that I leap on this type of imprecision because I want to exercise and show off my semantic proclivities, it's also because they lead people into confusion—people go off thinking "He said if one can be relatively objective, one should imagine that ..." and then one goes off, and if he's a respected intellectual figure or that sort of thing, you think "Well, he must know what he's talking about" and you sit there trying to work out what he is talking about, and not what the thing itself is about—so that you've really got what is a sort of veil between you and reality.

Q: How should one approach art? Sort of emotionally?

A: I think one should be, in relation to art—whether it be painting, sculpture and music, writing or whatever—open. That is not to say one should not have preconceived notions of any shape, form, proportion, this that and the other thing, because one has.

One should be aware that one needs certain terms of reference, but without becoming an expert and being able to discern each brushstroke and all that sort of thing, there are certain terms of reference which one can and is able quite naturally, and "natural" is the word, to apply. One can look at things within an organic context. Firstly, does one find a certain thing – either by shape or proportion or whatever – unbalanced or obnoxious or something like that? The use of colours in painting – are they harmonious or are they offensive?

Not again, saying "Well I mean there's purple and yellow side by side, it's sort of icky, yet so-and-so in his puce period painted it and I suppose it's all right." People will say, "Ah yes, art is subjective" – again, they're pulling it into that area. If there is such a thing as subjective art, by definition there must be objective art, therefore a painting or whatever it might be must conform to certain objective standards: proportion, colour, balance, and draughtsmanship and other things. You can't have subjectivity without objectivity.

You can say, "Ah yes, but some painters or some subjects I like, some forms of art I don't like." Now personally, I'm speaking personally, this is personal, it's not the subjective – I am a chocolate box pussycat man, I'm not cubist. I like Constable, Turner, da Vinci, I don't like … I can't remember their names – I don't remember the names of the cubists because I don't like them. If they are draughtsmen, for instance, and they honour and accept certain very reasonably accepted and established things: scale, proportion, and other things; and are prepared to be looked at, examined, or analysed both on the objective plane and the subjective – then fine.

If they're not, and they say: "Oh you don't understand and you're a Philistine" and this, that and the other thing – well, is there a problem? Basically one should approach art to look at it, to try and understand it, to appreciate it; not to force oneself unnecessarily into such a degree of appreciative function: "Unless you see a piece of art or something like that, and you get blown sky-high, you haven't appreciated it." *Because the impact of art, any art, can be immediate, and it can have a later relationship. The influence of it, the impact of it, however seemingly weak or strong, is always remembered if it has validity.*

This seems to be a big order, because one says, "Well, does that mean to say that every positive impact coming to any of the five senses, remains? – one retains that?" – the answer is yes.

Not all of it is retained in the conscious area, because there are different types of the memory-sense. There are the impacts which are in the forefront of the memory, which are the sort of immediate things that one needs and uses all the time, and there are banks of cells at the back which are, call it in the compressed form. They are a sort of historical archive, which remains. They are indexed, if you like. When they need to be pulled out to the front and put together with a similar type of positive, useful, valuable experience, contact or whatever – they slot in.

It would be an impossibility to keep turning over every possible piece of information, or every impact, all the time. Firstly, because there are many impacts which one does not consciously register as being of a positive nature. They can be very transitory, they can be "sleepers" which go in and are activated by contact with certain senses or with a situation at a later time.

Again, it comes down to the thing that if one alone had to accept or reject certain positive things, the margin of error would be too great. One could reject things which are useful, one could accept things which are negative or harmful in the guise of something which is acceptable, useful, normal, or seemingly positive – again, if one looks at art from an open point of view. Yet there is no danger that anything negative in its nature will have any lasting impact on one, or will get into the fundamental being.

One may see – one does all the time – in the guise of art, various things which are off-putting, or which one finds horrible or grotesque or nasty or something like that, and the surface impact is a negative one and one feels "Good Heavens, that's awful, isn't it?" Well, the worry of being influenced or impacted upon in a deeply negative way shouldn't be there, because it's a surface impact. But as to having an attitude towards art, well it's difficult to define it exactly, because it has a lot to do with mood.

So the thing is – have one's antennae reasonably aligned with certain varied points of reference, and by doing that one can fill in the other ones.

It's what we call the oil-spot technique: if you take a piece of paper and you put six or seven spots of oil in different parts – after a certain time they will coalesce, they will come together, they will creep through the paper and connect with each other.

So if one is first open, and one is aware, and the intention is there that one wants to profit from, benefit, develop knowledge of certain aspects of art – then this intention also fuels the ability to develop it. It needs a momentum to start, and it can be hard going in the beginning, but again it's like an enormous wheel; it needs a hell of a shove to get it started, but once it's going it just has to keep up a certain momentum.

So I think, basically, that one of the two cardinal rules of discernment, choice, between the so-called objective and subjective realities, as expounded by various philosophies, sometimes comes down to a very simple one: is he grinding an axe? What is his point of view, or what is his interest?

Okay, now this can be, of course, very complicated and it can be very confusing, and there can be a lot of false alarms or false starts, but in the beginning one should look at the surface implications. If, for instance, you go along and you want some information on a blood transfusion, and you go and it says "Doctor Dracula's Surgery." You go there and you will probably get a first-hand account of blood transfusion – is he for it or is he against it? He's for it! And it doesn't require very much wit or artifice to understand why he's in favour of it. Equally, you go to Jehovah's Witnesses and ask them; they're obviously going to be against it.

So what is the reality you've got? If you like, one says, "We don't approve of it" and the other says, "Objectively speaking, I think it's a marvelous idea!" If you like – it's a ridiculous example – it could be subjective or objective; but who do you ask? Dracula has an axe to grind, and the Jehovah's Witnesses have an axe to grind. The tendency is, again, to find the middle ground. And I mean, you cannot or you would not, hopefully, go around and ask the Jehovah's Witness who has protruding fangs, because his assessment of the situation would be, I am sure, very confusing.

He is trying to juggle with his desire to get his fangs into your jugular with the fact that he is a Jehovah's Witness and he shouldn't. He is terribly confused, so anything he is likely to say is likely to lead to more confusion. He is not by any means what might be called "in the middle" because he's got both problems. He is gone, like "gone" – because he's got too many problems. He's really "in it", as they say.

So. Also, any piece of art or writing, or any form of art or music — the appreciation of it or the impact that it has on a person is dependant on your mood.

It is also dependant sometimes on the intent or intention which is being imparted in it by the person who did it. For instance, there are some composers, who, way back, before it became known about brainwaves and things like that, put in certain beats which were brain rhythms. They induced certain states by getting the listeners' brain rhythms in step with the beat.

Chapter 7

REAL AND FICTITIOUS SPIRITUALITY

Reasons for stressing technical aspects rather than spiritual aspects of the Tradition to start with; Self-preparation; Avoiding conventionally spiritual concepts which narrow down the mind's focus; Enhanced perception; Avoidance of spiritual labeling; Using past situations to recreate a state; Mobilizing the energy-plus syndrome to build on past states or situations.

The codification of the spiritual and technical aspects of the Tradition is a very strong one and it is a kind of underlying tone to all activities.

However, the reason why one goes very deeply into the technicalities and the techniques to start with is because unless one can adequately master, or understand, or begin to understand techniques, with the intention of enhancing perception and feeling, and unless one is able then to use that hopefully enhanced perception, there is a risk that if, at the same time, a person is given or exposed to too much of a spiritual contact, there is a slight danger — although this also depends on personality and other things — that a person might overload the spiritual and say, "Yes, yes, the technical is all very well, but the spiritual is more rewarding."

I don't believe in taking any sort of risks. I believe in sort of a hundred and ten percent efficiency rather than hit-or-miss. So if one says, "No, no, I wouldn't do that," or "We wouldn't do that," the answer is that the intention may be there and may be very clear not to want to; but one has to take into consideration the attitude, conditioning, personality and other factors which can push a person into maybe trying too hard.

If it sounds as if the spiritual aspect is so awesome or overwhelming and frightening, or that people have to be prepared for the incredible shock or something like that — no. *The situation is that if one is being given contact, energy and spiritual values, one must be able to use them correctly, in the correct context, at the correct time, and with the correct feeling. They have to surface as a result of activities or exercises within the Tradition.*

A person prepares himself or herself to be able to benefit from a spiritual contact. Now, given that normal average conditioning immediately produces in people's minds ideas of what is meant by "spiritual" —what is meant by "spiritual contact?" What is meant by "spiritual experience?" What is meant by "spirituality?"

There is always a slight danger that a technique which a person learns, which enhances their perception—if that locks onto what they have conventionally learned as being "a spiritual experience", it may be wrong. I'm not saying "You discard any terms of reference or idea of what spirituality is, or what spiritual experience can be, because that's all eyewash ..." —no. It means looking at it and experiencing it in a different way, and more importantly, knowing what it means: fully experiencing it, not as a sort of sudden revelation or flash of lightening or anything like that—we don't and cannot depend on "hills and valleys" in terms of any sort of experience or development.

One starts off in very specific, quite mundane ways—how to sit, how to breathe, how to relax, what terms of reference to use, what to listen to. If the conventional learning factor comes in: "Yes, I've learnt that, now I want to use it—I've been learning that for three weeks or three months or three years, I want to use it *now...*" *—one can get into problems.*

One has to feel or know that one is capable of using a particular technique, and when. There is no such thing as a sort of time-table: "After x, y, or z time, a particular period is passed, a particular stage is reached."

Therefore there can be no matching together of the technical capacity or technical development, which is enhanced perception, with a "number one" spiritual-type thing—because in that area comes mechanicality: "I think I am prepared for a great experience;" "I would like to have a great experience," and then of course, "I need a great experience," "I want a great experience," or "I am ready for a great experience."

At some point a person has or feels a need, a desire, a requirement, an anxiety for some sort of spiritual guidance or awakening. They should not think that it is not there—if they said, "I wish it would happen to me" then you'd just have to say, "It wasn't until something else was established" —*because the underlying basis of the Tradition is development of a special nature as well. You see, one is by definition in contact with a great well, a great source or reservoir of spirituality. It is constantly there, it is constantly available, but it isn't communicated, or the communication doesn't happen, until a person is able to either use it or understand it, or understand what the contact means.* Otherwise, it's not that it would appear as some sort of terrible shock or frightening thing or something like that, it just would not be able to be understood and used usefully.

This is why there is so much emphasis in the Tradition put on learning the techniques; because in an activity —which might be an exercise of any nature, listening to a piece of music, meditating, doing an exercise —*in that state, a person is hopefully in a state of slightly higher perception. If they are in that state, it is technically only useful for them to be able to take on or absorb as much energy or knowledge as they can use in that state —plus a little bit more —which in fact they store for future situations.*

Fine. It would be not only inefficient but, in some cases, catastrophic from the point of view of confusion, if suddenly a great wodge of whatever were to descend on the person. It would confuse them, it would frighten them —not because it's frightening —but because they would think that they couldn't handle it and therefore something might happen, when in fact nothing would happen. But it would be inefficient.

So, one says that one talks to a person or people "according to the measure of their understanding" —right. Now that means exactly that. When one says one talks to the people according to the measure of their understanding, it doesn't only mean the verbal, it means that one communicates to people —whether it be verbally, whether it be tactile or whether it is by energy contact or whatever —it is only useful to that person if it is according to the measure of their capacity, not only to understand the communication, but also to use it.

There is no useful function at all performed if you are trying, for instance, to force a person. There's no such thing as putting a person in sort of a hot-house situation and pushing them in an unnatural way. Yes, under certain very extreme circumstances —if it is necessary, if it is desirable, if the person can take it—this is possible. But otherwise it is a dangerous experiment, because you can provoke all sorts of physical or psychological confusions and problems, the least of which is that the person starts blaming themselves, "I am so stupid I couldn't understand" or "I couldn't take advantage of all that, what does it all mean?"

So contact or communication is based on the capacity of the person, of the group, to use this usefully. Once a person, as a result of a contact, transfer of energy, exercise, or whatever, has experienced a state of being—they don't at that point have to put a label on it, they don't have to say "At that time I was in the sixth heaven," "seventh," "third," "second on the right," or what have you. All they have to do is to remember how they felt in that particular context, just as physically, for instance, after one has had a good meal, one has a distinct sensation that "that was a good meal." That's fine.

If one has had a sensation of this nature, you remember it, you file it. The next time you do a similar exercise or similar activity, you try and start on that level which you achieve—whatever you want to call it: state, level, thought, situation, it doesn't matter. You take it from that point, you recreate in yourself as closely as you can, the physical feeling or the ambiance or whatever you experienced at that last situation—and then you try and take it from there.

Because technically what happens is this: when I say that if you do an exercise or something, there is communication, there's a certain amount of energy; and the person receives energy compatible with the amount that they can handle at that moment, plus a little bit more. The "little bit more" is useful when they're trying to recreate that situation which they had before—the little bit extra which they have makes the bridge between that experience which they register, and they recall "It was like that. I would like to achieve the same situation"—fine.

That little bit of extra energy is the tangible link between the two situations, levels, or states. It's not just "saving it up because it's there" or something like that. Therefore if one can start establishing, and, which is more important, remembering a particular state of feeling or experience in a particular situation—and then doing an exercise or listening to something—you try and recreate that and aspire to reach at least an equivalent level of perception or openness. Not by any means sort of pushing it: "I will create such and such" because there you've got the tension factor coming in.

It should be "I have done it before. I remember what it was like, graphically, distinctly." So it was nothing "extra-terrestrial" that happened to me personally because I felt it, therefore I can feel it again, therefore I will try to increase it.

Again, one is not putting it in terms of an exact "sixth, seventh, eighth, ninth heaven" because one says "Right, that was a sixth heaven, I'll give it a bit of push and try the ninth, so that means I jump one" or "Maybe I can't jump one but if I fall short at least I'll end up in the eighth ..." and this becomes an end in itself. Many clairvoyants use this technique; and they say to you, "Ducky, I had a lovely vision for you" or whatever they say: "You nearly got to whatever" and that'll be fifty pence or whatever they charge now.

So you see, if you fall into the conditioned thing of "class one, class two; lesson one, lesson two, lesson three" you're saying "All right, I'll try and skip that" or "Maybe I can do it" or "Maybe I can't" and that can become somewhat daunting if the person has any doubt as to whether either intellectually or "x, y," or "z" they can do it, and therefore the intellectual measurement comes in and so forth, and you know, at that point forget it.

One has to say "This was the state" or "this is how I felt," however vaguely—"hot," "cold," this, that, something or other—"I will aim to start at that and push it up a little." How much, to which degree, what am I going to call it, it's the whole concept—yes. Because much has been said and continues to be said about things like "astral bodies" wandering about and so forth, and there is a great deal of imprecision about this kind of thing: "the astral body leaving the body," "the soul leaving the body," the "other being" wandering about somewhere or something. Now, whether this happens or not is, in fact, irrelevant. It can be a time-consuming thing: "Is that my astral body or is it something else?" and things like that.

This actually happens to people and they get preoccupied with all that stuff. I was in Manchester and I was waiting for a train, and next to the station there was this hall, and they were advertising "Astral Photography" and I went in and it was very interesting. It was warm — it was very cold in the station — and it was only fifty pence or something to have it done. They had a battery of cameras, and the people went up and sat on a thing, and they were told something by the astral photographer "to watch the astral" and he took a photograph. And that showed their astral body, or something like that.

Now if the phenomena actually exists that part of the consciousness actually leaves the human frame during a particular part of an exercise — this is irrelevant. If one says it does, this could disturb some people: "Supposing I was woken up suddenly, would it have enough time to get back?" or something; so why give people any more problems than they already imagine? During an exercise or an activity, what matters is the whole system. If one likes to make any sort of division between the physical or other self — I don't think it's useful. After all, people say, you know, "How cumbersome my physical senses/self is or this, that and the other thing"... well, it happens to be the only one one has at the moment.

However good the bottle is, it depends what is in it — whether the contents leave or not is not particularly important. What is important is that both the whole concept, the totality, should have the opportunity of contact in a particular exercise. If one limits it — either by reservation: "I will communicate with the left side of my brain and not the right" or "Is my left foot going to be influenced and not my right knee?" or something — this again can become: "Well, I don't see why it should be, could it?" — and it turns into a self-dialogue which isn't really useful.

If one accepts that the totality of the human framework is present at a particular time, which it should be — therefore it should be able to be communicated with on all those levels, within one's own capacity. Anything significantly greater than this capacity, doesn't damage, doesn't strain; but it produces, or can produce, either confusion or a feeling of doubt in oneself, or about what one is doing, or because one perhaps has decided what is going to happen. If it doesn't then happen, you get disappointment and everything.

As I've said before, one should be open to impact, which doesn't mean vulnerability. There is a delicate point here. The defense system comes into operation and it is a total defense against anything negative — it's not a defense against anything irrational, because the irrational is always present, so really it's just a disturbance factor — but anything of a distinctly negative character doesn't come in during that period. Enough comes in, plus a little bit more energy, plus another thing, what is called the "stretch factor."

The stretch factor means that during an activity or an exercise, a person may feel something, experience something, and they may feel that there is something just a little bit further away. Just a little bit. Not something vaguely "over there" but something just a little bit further. *It can be intangible, it's not very specific, but it encourages them to make a little bit more of an effort. It's slightly out of reach. They are encouraged to try for it because it is within their capacity.*

The use of this is that, having hopefully reached for it, aimed for it, and got hold of it; it is then a proof to them that the stretch factor exists, and that any limitation which they impose: "Oh no, I couldn't reach out as far as that" — is a self-imposed limitation; it's not an actual limitation. It's not the lollypop — you know, "Just 'get' that for once and for all and it'll be marvelous" — no. It's an ongoing thing, it's not a promise. It is a thing which a person can aspire to.

The human system is greatly under-considered, really, even though it can be abused, it can be polluted and goodness knows what. Nevertheless it doesn't lose certain very useful and fundamental abilities. One of them is that it has an extraordinary regenerative capacity, which shows itself in regenerating areas, which, because of conventional training, have not been exercised. If they haven't been exercised, they're not destroyed, but they have become stultified — they solidify in such a way that their elasticity is lost. Therefore if people are asked to use them, the automatic reply or reaction is: "Oh no, I couldn't aspire to that."

There is a great difference between aspiring to do something, and having too much ambition or greed. Ambition is a perfectly good thing, aspiring to do something is a perfectly good thing — overreaching and overbalancing is a completely different thing. "I want that" — now theoretically it's possible to do it. I shouldn't be influenced by what I think, if I want to pick a cup up without moving from this chair, what limitations does that impose on me? Well, the angle of the chair, when it reaches a certain degree — I'll fall on my face and that's not a very good idea. So therefore "what prevents me from sort of getting up and going over there and getting it?" One step at a time.

The moment you impose on yourself limitations which are a result of conditioning, then you have problems, and you have to go back and break down that conditioning.

Again, you don't break it down by a pitched battle, because than you are provoking conflict, the famous "battle within myself" and all that sort of thing. If, because of conditioning, you say "I don't think I can do that" or "I can't do that" — if it is something which is feasible and physically possible, fine — you can demonstrate that to this doubting or to this conditioned side of yourself. You demonstrate that it is possible — not in one jump, but little by little, or the assumption that, right, if I can move my hand six inches, there is every reason to suppose that I can also move it six feet along.

One is not overwhelming the conditioning, provoking a battle; one is undermining a conditioning by proof. Not "Well am I? ... No, I'm not" type of thing and then, "All right, we'll see" — because, don't forget, one can also, unknowingly, and certainly without wanting to, sabotage one's own efforts or activity. "I can't do it" — "Well, I'm going to do it" — and then one will probably do it, and do it badly, because the side of one which is conditioned hasn't backed one up, and therefore you think you can pick up that cup, all right, try it, pick it up and then — drop it. The sabotage factor has come in. That is the direct collision.

But if you say, "Well, to pick that up would mean that I have to move my hand like that, coordinate for distance, work out weight, flex the right muscles and so forth" — so I accept the fact that it's difficult or even impossible. However I'd like to try the first step, and the second step, and the third step, and the fourth step — when one eventually makes progress towards that, then the conditioned part of oneself, unless one is completely barmy, has to accept that this has happened — I mean that this is a fait accompli. So one says, "Right, I accept that I thought it was impossible, I have every reason to believe it was impossible, but I have proved it happened, so therefore that conditioning is not eradicated, it's just replaced by experience."

All these things relate to the very important aspect of spirituality and the spiritual contact, but a person shouldn't, also, be greedy, or frankly, over-enthusiastic about one's capacity to handle it. You know, "Sock it to me!" — "Tell me all about it!" and then "Bang!" and then they say, "Jesus, what happened?" — this is no big deal for anybody, and they will be the first to go whimpering off into the night saying, "What happened to me?" — and this is no useful function at all.

If a person is in a state where they can lift up, by development and perception, and then tame that perception for seconds, minutes — during that period of the heightened perception the spirituality communicates.

Like attracts like, and since spirituality is a fundamental part of the Tradition, development of techniques of awareness and openness must inevitably attract a development in the area of spirituality. Let's not get into an examination of which particular spirituality we're talking about; what degree, what aspect of religious experience one is aiming for and that sort of thing, because when it happens, a person is conscious of it.

They're not required to either develop stigmata, or go into some sort of "state" or something like that, because if the contact with the energy and the spirituality is working within them, any external phenomena which might manifest itself — unless it's useful — just doesn't happen within the Tradition, I mean except, literally, for theatrical effect, or to confound people or for any other justifiable reason — we don't have any of our Rumi, Hafiz, Jami or anything like that with the flashing lights coming out of their ears and floating around, or appearing through the walls ...well, appearing and disappearing, that's different. But I mean extraordinary things — except for this effect. And if that effect is implemented, it is usually not for any sort of teaching reason.

There are situations where a person might be in a situation, have an energy contact, produce energy in an activity or an exercise, and there might be a very minor quantity of excess energy. I'm not talking about the bridge energy which one would use in future occasions — I'm talking about a little bit of excess energy which might conceivably manifest itself physically.

It is not a sort of catatonic gnashing of teeth and then falling to the ground and everything like that — it just might be a sort of shiver or something like that. Now, if a person thinks that that was the experience, they would try to achieve a shiver again. So they'd get ice cubes, put them down their neck and shiver, and have a great "experience." But that was just an externalization, which is perfectly all right, perfectly reasonable, perfectly normal — but it's always the "I will do it, then I will put a mirror up there and look at myself and see if anything's happened."

Again, everybody's getting into the conventional area: "I feel terribly holy, let's see if there's a halo, no not quite, but not bad ..." If you're going on those terms you're setting yourself conventional levels and conventional measurements, and it is very simple to get disappointed in yourself, the Tradition, the technique or anything because "I've been doing the damned thing for five years and I'm not even a shadow of anything." And people can also, don't forget, go the other way and say, "Yes, could do with a little bit of polishing up, but not bad" – the other extreme.

Things cannot be measured in those areas. For too long people have tried to measure them; they've tried to codify them. They have, for instance, extracted esoteric experiences from writings from Muslim, Christian, Jewish and every other faith. "So-and-so experienced a transmogrification one day" – nobody ever says he'd been sweating over books and doing exercises for seventy years or something – and his transmogrification actually was because he tripped over a stone and fell over a precipice: he wasn't looking where he was going. There is a thing, I think it is a Spanish codex about the Jesuits allegedly martyred by the Moors. And it's a whole volume, and it's called ... *"Spiritual Heights and Spiritual Achievements of Jesuit Martyrs."* It merely is an index of things like, "I saw Saint Josephat and he was sitting there for fifteen minutes with a beautiful smile on his face" – finish. The volume is full of that. So does that mean that everybody should aim for sitting constantly with a happy smile on their face, and eventually being carried off to the nuthouse, *or should they aim to understand what could have created that smile on his face?*

All the functions on the different levels of perception hopefully develop in harmony with each other, and they must do, because if one area is developing inharmoniously, you get lack of balance. If you try, and if you could, concentrate specifically on one area to the detriment of others, then again you'd have a problem.

In a natural situation, a teaching has to take advantage of all the natural phenomena which exist, and all the techniques which will enhance and take advantage of those natural phenomena. We do not encourage people to think that they are becoming sort of possessed. What they're doing, if anything, is taking themselves over. They're taking themselves in hand rather than letting themselves run away, or worse, letting themselves be conditioned into a reactive state—which is perfectly all right, in some areas. As I say, certain points of conditioning are perfectly reasonable and natural and laudable, but it shouldn't be a press-button: you hear church bells, you fall on your knees immediately, no matter where you are. This is perfectly laudable in the right circumstances, I'm not knocking church bells or anything like that, but the situation would be wrong.

If a person is saying "I must think as a Jesuit father" or as John Knox or Rumi or anybody else at all—fine. But they should think like that, or learn to think like that because they want to understand how it works, not because "It is, therefore learn it." One has to liberate oneself—this isn't a liberation philosophy or anything—it's just that one is liberating oneself from, very often, self-imposed conditioning, and this really is some of the worst conditioning, because one is obviously close to oneself—therefore one is reminding oneself of one's conditioning all the time.

So one has to get away from it, and not battle with it. Benefit from all the influences and the energy—which abound.

Chapter 8

THE VARIOUS LEVELS OF DISCIPLINE AND INTENTION

Rejecting hard-and-fast concepts in favour of functional ones; Avoidance of tense applications; Keeping discipline protected from conditioning; Integrating one's own experience into discipline; Linking it consciously to the Tradition and letting it function; How ambition and aspiration should nevertheless exist; Defining one's energy-need and implementing it; How intention is indestructible; Stability and flexibility in action; How over-intellectualization can distort messages; How energy is passed on through positive activity; How communication is built up through people to increase the energy-flow.

Keeping one's aim defined is a constant repeating and reminding oneself of one's aim and intention – the use, direction, value, and various concepts – and the important thing is to realize first of all that when one is talking about concepts like this, we shouldn't be talking in an abstract sense.

Functional things like intention, energy, discipline are not things to which one says, "Yes, these are, if you like, 'Canons of the Law' – we pay lip service to them, and fine, let's get on with the nitty-gritty" – no. These are all functional aspects; they should be applied consistently and constantly. That, of course, does not imply looking for situations, circumstances under which to use one of these particular things all and every day for twenty-four hours – because this is a recipe for tension: "I am supposed to act like this and that" – "I am supposed to behave like this and that, therefore I will look constantly for possibilities and situations in order to use them."

What one wants to aim at is learning these concepts, learning how to apply them, and also how one applies them to oneself, taking into consideration one's own personality, upbringing, and various factors of one's own make-up which allow one to implement them using these factors.

That is to say: supposing one says, "Right, one of the concepts," shall we say, "is discipline." Discipline in the Tradition not only implies discipline of action, discipline of thought as well, discipline of intention: and how one exercises that discipline is also dependant on oneself, to the degree that discipline should not be subordinate to any conditioning or attitude that one has. It should not be imposed upon such conditioning or attitude, it should manifest itself through it.

If one was to take an example – it's a wild example but it'll do – supposing you say, "All right, I will be disciplined in action." In a Western concept and context, discipline of action implies a sort of precise militaristic or military bearing, tendency, thought or action. So if a woman decides that she will be disciplined in the way that she understands it, that would mean – illogically, but it happens – strutting about like a guardswoman or whatever, and this would be totally incorrect and unacceptable. But if the context of discipline is applied correctly, the person can say, "Right, if I'm supposed to discipline my actions, discipline should not mean robot or marionette-type activities." The best discipline is what's called a thinking discipline. Discipline which is merely a sort of gut-reaction or a sort of galvanic action as a result of a particular stimulus is not discipline, it's reaction. Discipline means that a person reacts to an instruction or an order based on the fact that they have absorbed a certain amount of terms of reference, so that they can, to a certain degree, understand what is implied by that order. Take what is commonly considered to be a very formal, strict, robot discipline and that sort of thing – military discipline – unthinking, unheeding, blind obedience. Well, I would not personally, as a soldier, like to command a unit which worked on the principle of blind obedience, because that is not the most useful thing at all.

Thinking obedience means this: if you give an order to a soldier to do something: "Now!" – the very fact that you have stars, bars or what have you on your shoulder, implies that you are capable and have been judged capable to give these orders – fine. The soldier obeys the orders, again, on the assumption that the officer knows what he's talking about, and that he wouldn't give the order unless he, as a soldier, was capable of carrying it out in the most efficient way without anybody suffering or getting unnecessarily killed.

In my book, that is not what is called "blind obedience." Thinking discipline is not the officer giving an order and then the soldier sitting down and thinking for fifteen minutes as to whether it's right, and "Oh, I don't know" and this, that and the other thing. No, he carries it out because he's been trained, hopefully, to carry out things.

If the order is "Scale that wall!" — hopefully he's been through an assault course or something like that — he knows how to do it. So he uses the discipline which he has learned to carry out an order. If it's carried out in a sense of absolute blind obedience: "I don't know what he's talking about, I don't know how to climb that wall but sure as hell I'm going to try!" — this is all very well and good, and it shows a certain amount of courage, application and so forth, but how much better is it to inculcate into a body of people or into a unit the knowledge that the people who are asked to do something are judged capable of doing it, and that therefore no sort of extreme knowledge is required of them in excess of that which they have either learnt or which they have read about.

So you don't start from zero.

A person will say for instance: disciplining one's actions means looking at one's actions, examining an area which one considers to be inefficient, ineffectual, less than desirable, and seeing what can be done about them. If what can be done about them is possible in terms of disciplining oneself, that is to say, "I have identified that I tend to eat cream buns or x, y, z and I put on weight" — cause and effect — "therefore since this is a personal indulgence, it is under my control and I should be able without great turmoil to reduce my intake of cream buns" — without recourse to anything terribly dramatic or involving other people.

If one identifies either a weakness or an area which one wants to develop, the same thing applies. You say "Okay, in a given circumstance I am unable to carry out a particular activity, or to think along some particular constructive lines, or indulge in some activity or area of thought which I consider, or is considered, valuable" — fine. One examines, again, carefully and with reasonable patience why one is not carrying these things out; or, if one is dissatisfied with the way one is carrying them out, how to carry them out better — because all these things are developmental. So you maybe try and analyse what the shortcomings are and recognize them, again, without being self-condemnatory — then see what one can do about it oneself.

If one finds, for instance, that there is an area of activity, thought of a developmental nature which one wants to boost up; to increase it — okay, fine. Now, one can give oneself a certain amount of this desired and required boost by working out how one can discipline one's thoughts, actions, readings or whatever, in order to facilitate this.

Additionally, having decided that one can marshall one's attention, one's concentration and one's thinking in a particular developmental path — this is where what we call the intention comes in. It is always valuable and usually necessary to repeat to oneself, to remind oneself of and refresh one's intention: "My intention is to do this." It's a calm, collected, un-tense, un-fraught decision. Having established the intention and cleared the decks for action, one then links that area of activity together with the energy of the Tradition; just as, in a very simple analogy, one gets a machine or a functioning thing. You overhaul it, you clean it, you put it in the best possible condition that you can, and then you give it the electricity, petrol or whatever energy it functions on best, and by an adjustment of the mixture screw or the high-tension or the low-tension or amperage or whatever, you get it functioning correctly.

Your specifying of your intention in an activity is the link between yourself and your activities in the Tradition.

You don't say, "Oh well, since I am in the Tradition, everything I do will automatically associate itself with it" — yes, to an extent. But how much better to make that very distinct affirmative move — to yourself. You don't shout it from the housetops; you don't necessarily have to let everybody know about it, but you repeat to yourself your intention, what you are trying to achieve.

Like attracts like. If you are directed correctly and you are functioning reasonably efficiently, the introduction of the energy into that circuit will fuel the system. It will also have a cleansing and rebuilding function — it's just as if you have a car engine or any internal combustion engine which has been lying idle for several weeks or several months or several years; it needs to be turned over by hand first with enough oil. Then, when you introduce the first combustion situation you get an awful lot of gunge and junk and ashes and old tin cans and so forth which have developed within the circuit, and which are blown out.

This is not a sort of esoteric purgative that I'm talking about, but what I am talking about is that there is a sort of inevitability about stop, start, and spluttering. The moment that one starts doing an activity one should hope for efficient functioning and tickover. If it doesn't happen immediately, one doesn't go barmy and run around saying, "It doesn't work, it's me, it's this, that and the other thing and so forth" — no. You examine the thing, avoiding the trap which one makes for oneself, that is: "I think" or "I heard" or "I understand" or "They say that this machine is capable of functioning at 5800 revolutions a minute." So therefore one starts it up, and your eyes are glued to some sort of gauge, and it doesn't make 5800, it goes up and it goes halfway and it gravitates and it splutters and then it goes back to zero, and you think "forget it."

Now in a very Neanderthal practical way, you'll drag a dirty old tractor out of a barn — nobody in their right mind expects that to start ticking over and answering to the accelerator sweetly the first hour or even the first day. True, you can go out and hit it with hammers and goodness knows what, but that doesn't mean to say it will work ...

Because if you aspire to something — this is perfectly all right. There should be ambition, aspiration, hope and all that sort of thing, because these things are fulfilled — but they're not fulfilled instantaneously. The person has to get used to that. Just again, the analogy of the car engine — if you start a car on a cold morning, you should, out of plain intelligence and economic sense, let it tick over for five minutes before you drive it away — in order that the lubrication should circulate, in order that the optimum temperature should be achieved.

What has that got to do with intention? What it has to do with intention is that if your intention, without excess haste, excess greed — greed takes on many forms, after all, it is not just food or power or money — greed is also haste, greed for time. "I will do this a bit faster and therefore the things will somehow get done faster" — no, it doesn't. If you push a thing beyond the level of its capacity, you're feeding it from below, but it is climbing up a sandhill. Certainly one is clawing back great quantities of sand, but one isn't in fact moving until the time comes that one stops and says, "Right, what is my intention? My intention is to climb over this sandhill. Right. Now let me look at this sandhill."

That is not to say that this is giving me the opportunity of being overawed by the size of the sandhill – no. It has been climbed – it can be climbed. Now, how do I climb it, based on my physical strength, ingenuity, and whatever other factors apply? You can try climbing straight up or you can take a diagonal path – a diagonal path doesn't seemingly get one up – but to go on a diagonal path is, in fact, the most efficient way of climbing a sandhill. If you look at it, you've got more and more sand under you each time on the diagonal. So if anybody remembers their theory of mechanics – the more pressure upwards underneath you, the more the platform is stable.

All right, this is not an abstract idea: "How does one climb a sandhill in an 'abstract' way?" Well the answer is you sit down and you think about it and then you work it out and you are no closer to the top of that sandhill after having worked it out. "Theoretically, one can do x, y or z" – theoretically one can do a lot of things, but is the satisfaction not greater, and the impact and the experience much greater, if it was done in a practical way?

If one is conscious of one's intention – not sitting like a vulture on one's shoulder picking at one's ear and making one feel uncomfortable all the time – no. But repeating it in areas, situations which one considers to be valuable, viable, and requiring a relationship with, and a jolt of energy from, the Tradition. One has not only the right to expect this energy and the need to have that energy, but one has a responsibility to ask for that energy. A lot of people – understandably, sometimes – feel hesitant: "Oh, do I have the right?" "Oh, it might be wasted" "Oh, maybe somebody else needs it."

Well, all these possibilities are there, but the defense mechanism operates more simply, because there is not an inexhaustible quantity of energy available for each region. If you have everybody involved in the Tradition in one particular region asking for energy under every circumstance – "Oh, I just need a boost to catch that bus" and "I am going out, I'll need a boost of energy so I'll not forget anything when I go out" – this energy could be drained very quickly. So the fact that one asks for that energy does not necessarily mean that one receives it.

There are, after all, priorities. I know what the priorities are, and I'm certainly not about to tell anybody — so don't worry about that.

The priorities may seem difficult to imagine, so don't try and "work them out" because it is difficult to imagine what the priorities are, because they are dependant upon the time, the place and the need.

The time, the place and the need, in a given circumstance, can only be seen over a whole area, in certain dimensions. They cannot be seen from one side; so it is like — if you can imagine a chessboard made out of glass with black and white squares, and imagine, for instance, thirty chessboards, one exactly on top of the other, and the same number of chesspieces on each board.

Right. Now you have 36 times 36 to the power of 6 possibilities, 90,000 to 1 against you being able to move one piece into a square which is not occupied on any of the other levels. So you say fine, well in that case I'm not going to play the game, because this is ridiculous.

The answer is, and this is why I say do not worry about the priorities, because you know, if you're looking down to 30 chessboards, after a time — I assure you, out of experience, that sometimes you think: forget it, no way. But of course — to mix metaphors somewhat — the joker in the pack is the fact that there is one blank chessboard. Now those of you who are chess fiends know that if you have 30 chessboards, and you had a full set of pieces on each chessboard, it's literally impossible to move a piece on any other chessboard. However, if you put a completely blank chessboard at a particular point, you then have a 30 to 1 change of moving a piece without it being in an occupied square.

If this is becoming too complicated: just listen to the rest. If you have 2 chessboards, you've got a 15 to 1 chance: with each further move, it gets progressively more difficult. Now in order to avoid the practical fear, dread, confusion and horror which the average person would suffer from by looking at that and thinking "this is impossible" — one doesn't have to worry about it. That is, if you like, the only area — or not the only area but one of the only areas which, I can assure you, can remain as far as you're concerned, "in the abstract." Just let it be said that is that.

I neither have the time nor certainly the inclination to explain it. Just let us say: it exists. So the only way it can exist and the only way it can function — that is, it can exist, but it can't function without the blank board.

Now what has that got to do with intention? What it's got to do with intention is this: that if you're intention is that this is an activity — it's a practical activity, it's not a game. Chess is a game, chess is a pastime — yes, certainly it can be such. Originally, it wasn't, and it has a very strong multi-dimensional aspect, and of course it has the enormously strict disciplines of the game. You either move like this or that, or you don't. You can't say, "Well, I think today I'll move the knight in diagonals," because that is not the thing. But also, thinking ahead, you're not only working out what the other side can do, you're working your moves out, based on the tactics and stratagems employed by that person — basing your knowledge of them.

What does it teach you in actual life? What it teaches you is this: what one might call the imponderables — though it's the opposite numbers who are, if you like imponderables — not people but situations.

These situations are capable of developing in almost any direction. It is conceivable for instance that one says, "Right, I have a situation which is coming up. I am taking a bundle of clothes to the dry cleaners." Right — now that's a situation, okay? Predictably one will go to the dry cleaners and one would go in and one would hand the stuff over and one will get a ticket and they'll tell you, "Come back next Tuesday," or whatever, and you will leave. It doesn't require what one would call "in-depth planning" to do that. You do all the things which build up to the successful conclusion, and you're intention is to take those clothes and get them cleaned.

Now every action and thought which goes toward the successful culmination of that action should be carried out. It implies rudimentary things like getting up in the morning, dressing, having breakfast, getting the stuff together, going out, locking the door, going to the place, giving it to them; speaking to them in a coherent language. You might say: "Well, it's obvious, one does it" — yes. That is a very simple thing. Every activity ahead of one during the day is not quite as predictable as that, but the mechanics of activities are, if they are laid out as far as one can see. Now, you are not in control of that situation; there are imponderables. You could go into the shop and, having hopefully got up and dressed, had breakfast and so on, made your way to the shop, found that it's nine o'clock, that it's open, handed the stuff over to the woman behind the counter—who had then gone raving mad and torn it to pieces.

And you think, "Ooh, I think something is wrong. I have the best intention in the world; look at this lunatic woman—she has destroyed my intention." Yes, she has torn your clothes—but does that do anything about destroying your intention? The answer is no. Do you then say, "All right, I'm going to go to the cleaners but I don't think I'll go because this might be one of her mad days and I'll go along the next day or I'll send somebody in to see whether she's mad and if she's not then I'll sneak in quickly before she goes mad" or something. Well, this is a very time-consuming way of carrying on—however, people do it.

If I use the analogy of the chess game: before the game starts, the pieces are lined up. One knows the rules of the game first. One knows the aim of the opponent; one knows one's own aim—right. In the normal game of chess the person will open with the pawn, and then a particular stylized opening—right. However, there are possibilities that instead of opening with the pawns which are the front rank, somebody might feel funny and open with a knight, which jumps over the pawn. You then don't rush screaming into the darkness or whatever because that wasn't a correct opening or "What does this mean?" or "Goodness, there go my plans" because they hinge on that fellow using the "Roy-Lopez opening" or whatever.

Just as there are imponderables in situations in the future, that doesn't mean to say that one's reaction should be equally imponderable—that is, hidden from oneself—otherwise one is a complete morass. It doesn't also mean that one is so fraught with latent dangers that may happen, that one doesn't go to the cleaners in case they say, "Yes, Madam," take your garments and set fire to them—"So I think I will dress myself in asbestos or take asbestos clothes, or not go to that person, or stay in bed all day." You say, "No, no, that's ridiculous" but people do those ridiculous things.

In answer to a chess move or an unpredictable move in a situation—as long as one has maintained stability, flexibility, one then has seconds, sometimes minutes, sometimes hours, sometimes days, to react—but whatever one's reaction is to that circumstance or that situation, it should be a thinking one; it should be one which is a reasonably balanced and disciplined one, having repeated to oneself what one's intention is in getting involved in the situation.

Then, having done one's homework as far as one thinks and hopes one has, one can invoke or involve the energy of the Tradition to push forward one's intention in a valuable way. How much energy – under which circumstances – over these circumstances, one has no control. You can't say, "Well I need, you know, 75 pence worth of energy" or something like that. One can't debate interminably: "Can I or do I have the right to?" – no, assuming it's a reasonably significantly important thing. That doesn't mean to say by any means that it's something of such "transcendental" importance – no, it can be perhaps an insignificant thing. It can be an insignificant thing to other people: if, for whatever reasons, it is significant enough for oneself, then one should tackle it.

If it is something with enough nuisance value or disruptive value, one should do something about it. In circumstances like that one has every right, reason and justification to say, "Right, I need to lock into the energy of the Tradition in order to produce an effect." As I say, by making that statement, by making that decision, it doesn't mean one automatically gets it; but it does mean that if it is made available to one, and that the activity can be carried out in a more efficient and beneficial way for all the circumstances and the person involved.

Sometimes – and I say sometimes because it is sometimes, and I have no intention of saying which are the sometimes and which aren't the sometimes – the energy which a person might need or ask for in a given circumstance doesn't come in the way they imagine it will come, or would like it to come, or in which they think it would come. In some circumstances, we are very – the word "crafty" has been applied – I don't necessarily appreciate this idea because it's more than crafty, but anyway – one looks to the circumstance and one lets the person get on with it.

Now is that harsh, cruel, horrid – "We didn't help them," "We didn't push them," and that sort of thing? Not at all. It is either because in actual fact they can do it themselves – they're asking for a push, help, energy and so forth; they achieve something – right. They may think, "Well, thank goodness I went through the motions, I remembered to affirm by decision and with a little bit of push, I got over it."

Now, isn't this dishonest? Aren't you telling them that something is available and then when they ask for it, not giving it to them, and they achieve it anyway and they give you the credit? It would be dishonest if you left them to believe that – but you don't. What you do is you get a situation where you say to them: "That worked quite well," or "That wasn't too bad" or something like that, and they feel happy or glad that it has worked, and then, either in a direct or roundabout way, you tell them: Well you did that, you know.

You used the terms of reference, you used the tactics, you used the mechanism when you did it. If you did it: you can do it better. You achieved something which wasn't the result of a sort of shoring-up technique – no. You used the technique; it worked. And then you get maybe a little bit snide and say: But don't think that you don't need backup, which is there when you need it.

So there are multiple facets, insofar as you can't demand energy – but you have the right to ask for it. You can't judge how much you need, but the right quantity is available, and that is a tangible thing, it's neither theoretical nor abstract, nor is it anybody's gift in the sense that one thinks: "Oh, poor so-and-so, he's been slogging away a bit, I'll throw him a few oats" or something like that – no.

Because if I'm doing anything, I'm almost detached from the situation in the sense that I'm almost disinterested. Almost. That again, is not the sort of puppet-master thing that it sounds like, or a sort of clinical detachment – no. Again, it's not the over-involvement and it doesn't lead to indulgence – either because one likes or dislikes a particular person, or one sees a person in a mess that they're making and one says, "Right, they'd better learn from ..." No. Unnecessary suffering is unnecessary. Unnecessary conflict and confusion within a person is unnecessary – I don't believe and we don't believe in this famous "catharsis" where people tear themselves to pieces and emerge greater and better. In my experience this so-called catharsis causes a lot of confusion, suffering to family, friends and so forth – and all right, a person emerges nobler and chastened – but it can be done much more efficiently.

It's just like these unfortunate "Hindu mystics" – and you see them wandering about India – who have held their arms up until they are atrophied, and the great thing there is: the birds have nested, literally, in the palm — and this is mind over matter. They say, for instance, one shouldn't knock this, because it shows devotion, sense of purpose and that sort of thing. As far as I'm concerned it's a damned waste of a perfectly good limb, which other people could have used. If it were possible to chop that off and give it to somebody who needs it, that would be a far greater thing than having a bird nest in your hand, however much you like birds.

If you can, use the amount of discipline, which I admit is enormous — not to mention the amount of energy, discipline, character — in a functional way, in such a way that they don't have to prove to themselves by mortifying the flesh that they're capable of doing it; but just accept it as being a fact. I mean, how much energy is generated by sitting on beds of nails? How much discomfort does a person suffer in order to conquer the plain pain and anguish? I maintain that their energy should be used in a constructive way — to them it may be constructive — but we are not engaged in a passive activity. We're engaged in a positively demonstrably developmental and useful activity.

Yes, we are all subordinate to certain forces. Yes, it is possible to walk on coals, stick knives in your cheeks, sit on beds of nails — a fellow in Delhi sat on top of a pillar for days without eating until he fell asleep and fell off — and that proved the fact that gravity exists. It also orphaned his three children, which I'm sure they had reason to bless him for.

But if one is accused of knocking people for doing this sort of thing — yes, I do. Because I think an activity like that can be channelled — if the intention is aligned. For instance, those people in Persia who stick things through themselves on the tenth of Maharam — not to put too fine a point on it: they are bananas. Really. It takes discipline to do that. Now in my terms and to my mind, in a normally balanced human being this self-immolation or any of that kind of thing, causes and must cause a great inner strife. I don't think it solves anything, because the very fact that it is my intention to drive a spike through my nose or whatever is acting contrary to the basic need of the human being, which is survival. This is aggressing against survival. So therefore you are surely putting yourself against yourself.

If you will say, right, there are certain areas in myself — laziness, greed, stupidity, x, y, z and so forth, which I want to master, control, eradicate and fix onto a developmentally useful pattern and push those. In no way do I see a collision, as there is in that type of spiking the nose and piercing the cheeks. To conquer something is also to harness oneself to the fundamental basic energies and qualities of the human being, which is itself harnessed to something.

All right, you're proving something: "All right, I'll stick a thing through my nose, I have proved that I can do it and I can go into some sort of hypnotic state or something like that and do it, and it won't hurt." It doesn't hurt when you do it because the pain sense in the cerebellum is a very simple thing: it feels pain and it stimulates a reflex, which is tensing up or screaming or something like that – you can get yourself into a state, eat hot coals or what have you, and not feel a thing – but afterwards, in no way is that piece of broken glass or what have you stuck through their nose not going to hurt.

So basically, what I think is that this is a waste. I'm against any form of mortification of the flesh, either to show off, or as a circus act, or to show at that instant that one can so desensitize the pain centre that one can do it easily. It can be done, it has been done – I dare say that people have been capering about like that for a long time.

Why not accept the fact that there is an intention, an energy, a quality which has been used in doing that, and why not harness that intention to something useful, rather than wandering about with a piece of exhaust pipe stuck in your nose? I think this is an abuse of the body; it's an abuse of the function which one should use to a purpose. If one believes strongly enough that a discipline can allow one to do it, then take it from there – you don't have to prove it unless you have to. And I'm afraid I think that if you have to prove it, it means you're not quite sure whether you can do it.

But as I say, I've questioned these gentlemen, and they confess that it is very painful. And I think it is not useful. The intention is good; the energy to do it is there; the intent is to prove something – okay. Supposing you take it as read that the intention and the discipline will carry you through. I maintain that it is not necessary to have to go through the physical anguish of proving it. "Oh, I won't go on unless I can demonstrate to myself that I can do it." Why not take it as read, and say "Okay, I think I can do it – I may need a bit of backup." That is where the energy of the Tradition comes in. Then one says, "Okay, now I'm going to do a certain thing, I want to achieve it, I think it's useful, I think it's beneficial, I think it's developmental, I think I need a bit of a push."

Now this is no admission of weakness or whatever. A reasonably responsible thinking person takes advantage of other people's knowledge, construction and development, every day, without hesitation. Gottlieb Daimler — or whoever it was who invented the internal combustion engine — invented it, and it has then been developed by others. When you drive and when you take a taxi or a bus or something like that, you're taking advantage of somebody else's invention, somebody's development, capital investment by people to build factories to produce cars — and you do it without hesitation. You don't feel any anguish: "Oh, shall I take advantage of Gottlieb Daimler's invention?"

Certainly, if you go out and pinch his invention and register it in your own name or something like that, that's a completely different thing. But people do take advantage all the time in every way — not in a bad way — but they make use of other people's inventions without a qualm.

So why not, in the Tradition, take advantage and make use of the activities, the actions, the writings, and the techniques which have been produced specifically with the controlled and balanced development of persons in mind?

They were not written down as abstract theory — they were not written down to show how clever people were, because they are too concise in their directions. They're not airy-fairy. All you have to do is to read some of the lives and some of the histories or some of the sayings or actions of people like Jami, Hafiz, Rumi, Saadi and others, and you will find that they were eminently down-to-earth, in the sense that they said things which were readily or soon understandable. They spoke in the parlance of the context in which they lived, and if their phrases are a little bit updated, they are eminently workable in the present day.

With people who have tried to look at Rumi and his voluminous writings, certain professional esotericists, intellectual esotericists and birds of that feather have gone through his books, and in some areas they've been terribly foxed by some of the terms, phrases, language, and other things which he used. You would have thought that if a person is supposed to be an intellectual and he is writing a commentary on Rumi's speeches, you might consider that he is reasonably intelligent.

One fellow – a Persian – was foxed by one of the passages, which is a record written by Rumi – it's part of the Mathnavi – when he writes down, in the form of a diary, just a daily interchange between himself and some students, a question and answer discussion sort of thing – and this completely foxed this fellow. He had forgotten one very fundamental thing, that Rumi was born in Ralkh, which is in Afghanistan – he came from an Afghan family. Chunks of the Mathnavi are written in Dari, which is Afghan Persian. It is very old Persian, the original Persian; and to a present-day Persian, it reads rather like Chaucerian English to a present-day English writer.

And they're completely fooled by it; they can't understand it, because they say to themselves, "Oh, this is a very primitive Persian, but we can't say that because if you say that Rumi was primitive, that's nasty, one shouldn't say that about him" – He wasn't being primitive, he was being a Balkhi. The rest of the Mathnavi is written in the classical Persian, if you like, but for instance when he writes – and this is a great source of amusement to some of us who read it in the original: in the expurgated version which was available in Persia, published by the University of Teheran – there are chunks missing.

One of the chunks which is missing is very funny because it is a thing which Rumi wrote and he says something like, "I was sitting at such-and-such a place and somebody came up to me and said: 'Are you Rumi?' and I said 'Sometimes,' and he said, 'Well, I'd like to ask you a question,' and he asked me a question of such absolute garbage and stupidity that I became incensed and I took off my slipper and chased him down the street, beating him the while."

That is expurgated, because they say: "Soul of patience," you know, "wouldn't have done that," "learned man" and so forth – he was an Afghan, and he lost his cool in the face of this blithering idiot who had buttonholed him rudely without saying, "Excuse me," or the normal courtesy, which is sitting down for a few minutes and grasping at the tactic to open a conversation. Supposing Rumi or anybody was holding forth, and he mentioned anything. It is the sort of conversation gambit: if he says, "Oh, I remember when I was attacked by a vulture," or something – the fellow says, "Vulture, yes, my mother used to tell me about vultures," and so forth; so he's got the conversation for a few minutes. This is a politeness. You don't say, "Just a minute! What's all this about vultures?" — you wait for a moment.

So you don't go out and buttonhole a fellow and say, "Oh, you're Rumi aren't you?" — this is an absolutely ridiculous fool. So Rumi reacted in a perfectly normal way. And they take this out, because this apparently shows Rumi in an unfavourable light.

But the point is, they have missed the fact that he was an Afghan so therefore it was an Afghan dialogue. His reaction was perfectly Afghan, and after all, he was flesh and blood, and he was not the sort of person who would sit there and say, "Yes, that is the most marvelous question," and "I think you've got to come back in 30 years," or something like that. He just thought "The only way to teach this fool a lesson is to give him a good thumping," which he then did.

I have seen this — and never mind about it being written down and well-annotated by himself and his students and people like that — but I have seen my own father and my grandfather acting in not dissimilar ways with particularly annoying people; and I remember from the time I was very small thinking "Good Heavens!" I remember my immediate reaction was "You'd better watch it" because obviously you always think of it in relation to yourself — and then I used to think, "I wonder why?" and sometimes I would ask my father, "Why did Grandfather …?" Once I asked him, "Why did Grandfather beat that fellow?" and he said, "Well, because I wasn't near enough to get him, because I would have liked to have beaten him as well." Or, alternatively, "Why did he clip that fellow around the ear?" And he said once, "Because I wasn't near enough to get the clip" — and so it works in all directions.

What all that has to do with intention is that if a person has got the priorities of their intention reasonably right, reasonably in order, they are guided reasonably by those intentions.

When I talk about priorities, don't forget that priorities can also be arranged or rearranged or modified according to circumstances. They're not so rigid that a person, say, goes through a list of priorities and willy-nilly they stick to those.

If there's an unexpected thing, then that unexpected thing should be compared with the priority. If it is obvious — a risk to life, limb and all that sort of thing — this is a significant priority. So one shouldn't then say, "No, this is my day for polishing the brass and I don't care if the termites are eating the foundations." You will rue the day, if you polish the brass.

It's not "Shall I polish the brass or get rid of the termites?" If the intention is correct to maintain the house in good order in order to keep your brassware and so forth, then the priorities are self-delineated, and it is not such a tremendous intellectual or mental gymnastic to arrange one's priorities in a reasonable way.

It is very tempting to arrange them and rearrange them daily, according to either one's preference or one's hopes or one's fears. There's nothing particularly wrong in that, provided the priorities are not continually changing in a significant way, because then you get sort of priorities jockeying for position, one against the other, one pushing the other one: "Yes, I want this but I need that," "I think this, but somebody says that," and then you get into the unenviable position of being your own umpire, and that is a position which one can do without.

People try to do it, you know, things like, "I should be able to work this out" — certainly, but again there's nothing wrong with saying, "My intention is to work this out and use tactics, techniques, terms of reference, thought and energy which are available." There is no great benefit in saying, "I won't ask for energy, help, etc. — I'll do it myself." Certainly, a person should be encouraged to try and do things themselves with a bit of help, within a context. It doesn't in any sense make them reliant; nobody's going to call in the debt — you know, "Knock, knock, I remember when you had a bit of a problem and we happened to help you and now you do me a favour" — no. Nobody owes anybody a thing in that way.

If you do somebody a favour — I don't like the word "favour" because it has implications — if one does something in a way that one helps somebody else, that is an investment of positive energy; and the hope is that that person will then pass that on when they have the opportunity. Nobody has a lien on help because then it's not help; it's a qualified help. You go to the bank and say, "Lend me five hundred pounds," and they say, "Fine, at x percent" — this is a normal commercial activity; banks wouldn't exist very long if they didn't do that.

In the aspects of the developmental pattern, if you start something going with the correct intention, it's like in the Tradition we use what we

call "secret charity." People are given money or help or whatever and they
are expected to then, when and as and if it is possible for them, to help
somebody in turn; then the energy goes on because the intention was the
momentum — which may end up goodness knows where. One doesn't
control it, one can't control it, one isn't expecting the immediate come-
back, because it's an investment of energy.

The intention goes along with everything. An action started with a
fundamentally bad intention, that is, a negative intention, can go along
for years; but inevitably at a certain time, when the person or whatever
it is who has invested this bad intention — at the moment when they can
least take it — in that circumstance, the debt is called in. And Bang! —
"What did I do?" — "Think."

So that should give you something to chew on. But as I say, one
should be reasonable. You don't sort of psych yourself up. Everybody
has their own way of communicating, talking to themselves and express-
ing their intention to themselves: "I want to do this because it is beneficial to myself, the context, the group, person, whatever. It is
developmentally useful and I think I should do it; I believe I should do
it" and then you go ahead and do it.

The abstract — if you look at it from the simple point of view — in
terms of history, the abstract has never survived. It's the tangible and
experiential which has survived. That doesn't mean to say that abstract
artists haven't made billions out of their abstract art, and that has in
turn fueled real estate or whatever they bought with the money which
in turn provided jobs — it's all right, I suppose ... but when it gets to the
soup of the soup, the fellow who is tilling the soil, does he give thanks
to the abstract artist? — No, because the abstract isn't tangible enough
to him.

But if the intention is that one of the threads — we're talking about
communication — we're talking about building up threads of communica-
tion, lines of communication, which can take more and more energy, ex-
change of energy, and influence and develop a person within the context
of that increased familiarity and increased contact and communication
with themselves. That is no way-out thing.

Preface all activities, as far as possible, with intention. Every exercise in the Tradition should be prefaced with an intention. If there is an
expressed intention, the affirmative "I intend to do the exercise or

whatever, for the purpose of ..." This can be precise: it can be in the form, for instance, that we use sometimes for sending energy to a place, a person, or a situation – or it can be, again, not abstract but slightly less precise in the sense that "I am doing this exercise for a developmental purpose – mine, somebody else's" – it doesn't matter, as long as it's pointed in the right direction.

Chapter 9

SPIRITUALITY AS A BASIC REQUIREMENT

Avoiding intellectualizing it; How spirituality encompasses the mind, being, context, life, belief; External spirituality as opposed to internal; How development bases itself on relationship; Applying spirituality practically; Intelligent enhancement of spiritual situations; Freedom as lack of choice; Role of affirmation; Avoiding blame; Focusing by incorporating context rather than by ignoring it.

As you all hopefully know by now, I've explained and detailed many of the aspects, techniques, terms of reference of the Tradition — and from time to time I have also mentioned an aspect which is of considerable importance, and towards which and in the context of which we work — and that of course is the aspect of spirituality.

Is spirituality a state of mind, a state of being, a term of reference, a way of living, or does it encompass belief? Spirituality in the best, most harmonious and balanced sense, incorporates all of these. Spirituality relies on the existence of a fundamental belief — right. From that fundamental belief stems the practicality of the use of spirituality.

A person is not a machine in the sense that they have graduations, and they have little things which are marked "spirituality," "being spiritual," "feeling spiritual," "using spirituality," and they switch one off and the other one on — they live within the whole context and they apply spirituality in the context in which they find themselves at a given time.

A person can feel spiritual, think spiritually, react spiritually, without showing any necessary manifestation of spirituality. Because after all, define what is, if you like, a show of spirituality.

Certain countries, certain cultures, define outward spirituality in different ways. Whether it is wearing a patched robe to show that one is poor, or whether it's wearing a monk's habit and carrying a crucifix, or using a tasbee, or shaving one's head, or wearing different robes, all that sort of thing—different cultures therefore define outward spirituality in different ways.

Can one therefore say, there should be a homogeneous exteriorization of spirituality? And I think, from the point of view of the Tradition, that the answer is no.

If you want to harmonize in the exterior way, either by behaviour or by dress, you would have to incorporate all the signs and symbolisms of the different religions or different cultures, which, to them, imply a spiritual relationship. It could be a Buddhist's robe, a tasbee, a crucifix, a shaven head, this, that and the other thing. Apart from the fact that this would be fairly ridiculous-looking, certain of the aspects indicated externally by various articles or instruments must necessarily be in conflict on that level.

"The Cross against the Crescent," the this against the that — externally. Now, on an external level, one doesn't have to necessarily manifest one's spiritual adherence. In certain contexts, it is required; in certain contexts it is necessary, in certain places, this is valuable and there is no objection to doing it. If a person, for instance, goes on the Haj, there is a very specific costume which is dictated, which is to be worn. It is a very simple garment—for instance, for a man it is two garments, it's the equivalent of two large bath towels—one is worn around the waist, one is worn over the shoulder. It is the sign of poverty, and everybody wears the same, so there is no difference whether the man is a king or a beggar.

This is a sign of equality, it's a sign of humility, it is a traditional thing to wear. It is worn only in Mecca during the Haj. A person does not wear it anywhere else to show that they have been on the Haj. It is not an outward sign of spirituality. You can wear it, I suppose, theoretically—there's nothing to stop you, except yourself, from wearing it in the street. It would be considered to be incorrect, it would be considered to be showing-off, and one would probably get into trouble for wearing it. Wearing it does not give a person spirituality. It is an outward garment. It is correct, it is normal, it is required, it is necessary—under those circumstances. Just as normally, a woman who goes into a church or something, covers the head. This is perfectly normal. This is a demonstration of adherence to a spiritual situation; it is not a measure of the person's internal spirituality.

Spirituality can be a way of life, in the sense that a person can devote all their time, all their activities, all their efforts, everything, in a search for developing, increasing and deepening their feeling of spirituality. In some cultures this implies living in a cave in a mountain or doing things like rejecting the world, abandoning everything, meditating constantly, eating almost nothing or very little, and by this way hopefully developing a spirituality.

We hold that this is incorrect, because this is not a balanced or harmonious activity. Even if it satisfies the person themselves, that they feel more spiritual, closer to God by rejecting the world and so forth, I think that their attitude is not correctly balanced.

Everybody somewhere, somehow, has somebody to whom they are related, who cares for them, who wants them, who needs them — they have a place in a family, in society — they have a function which they can and should perform as much as possible. They may say, "Yes, my function is to increase my spirituality, and I am helping this civilization or town or village, or whatever it may be, by sitting in this hole in the mountain and developing my spirituality. This is my participation." Well, I speak as a Muslim — and "there is no monasticism in Islam" — but I think that it's not correct, for the simple reason that it is too easy, in a way. I'm not saying it's too easy in the sense that everybody's going to rush out and climb into cages and sit there and — Bing! Sudden illumination — no, it is too easy in the sense that it is not so much of a problem to live. A person doing that is in fact abdicating their responsibility towards themselves and other people.

All right, they are no longer being tested by the fact that they have to earn their living, pay their telephone bill otherwise they'll be cut off, or pay their road tax, or do whatever — they don't need these problems — right. If you look at it a reasonably balanced situation, it is not that much of a problem to pay one's road tax or to pay one's telephone bill, however reluctant one may be to do so.

And I agree with the reluctance, but, nevertheless these are certain things which are manageable. If one cannot afford to pay such a large telephone bill, it is perfectly possible to make less telephone calls. This is not such an obnoxious limitation on one's liberty or one's personality or being or whatever. So therefore when I say it is easier — it is easier possibly if one is that way inclined — to live in a cave and talk with ravens or whoever inhabit the local caves; but it is not the easy — it is not the royal road, the golden way to spirituality.

In fact — and I don't suggest that anybody tries it — go and spend five or ten or fifteen years in a cave, and get all spiritual, and then come down and go about and say "Hallelujah" or whatever people say after fifteen years in caves, and men in white coats will come and take you away.

It is no good saying, "I am all spiritual" and that sort of thing, because they say, "Yes, yes," and they give you a shot and calm you down. So what have you achieved? Notoriety, possibly, but little else. Self-satisfaction? — "Look at these people, they don't appreciate me" — I've been saying that for years and nothing has changed. So if you are doing it for self-satisfaction, that cannot be equated with spirituality. *It is much more functionally useful, positively useful, to a person themselves, to their family, to their friends, to their society — and cosmologically speaking — to develop a spirituality within the context in which one exists.*

The basic impulse to develop a spirituality, a knowledge or feeling of one's place in the universe, one's relation with man, with God, and so forth — that is the basis.

From that comes the practical application of learning, technique, development. This is where the Tradition comes in: because it aims to teach, to instruct, to make available to people ways, means, techniques, texts, information or whatever; so that not only can they work at increasing the awareness of spirituality, but actually become able to feel it as well as use it. I think it can best be used when it becomes familiar. Now there's a saying in English that "familiarity breeds contempt." Possibly, in some areas — what it means is that when one becomes more used to a thing one possibly takes less care of it. This certainly shouldn't be so in the sense of increasing one's awareness — spiritual or deep awareness. When aspects or points of view of spirituality become familiar, one uses them more frequently and they mean more to one.

They are not something which is borrowed or something which is put on for the moment, "Oh, I'm being spiritual for the next five minutes, right," and so forth. Unless one feels it, unless one uses it, and unless one literally revels in it, really feels — I won't say exalted, because that sort of presupposes a "zap" sort of exaltation — no. But a feeling, yes — a warm feeling, if you like.

So, as I say, it's not the switch-on, switch-off, 2 degrees, 5 degrees, 10 degrees – it is building up a threshold, and then an awareness, and a feeling of spirituality through achievement. The achievement is not a predetermined thing: you know, Saint Mark 9, Saint Mark 8 and Saint Mark 7, and then Saint Mark 1b for the big one – spirituality is a thing which a person feels themselves. They work on themselves. The spirituality is gauged, judged, stimulated, and in some cases dampened, by the person who is teaching, because it is his function to measure it and see in which way it can be best used by the person, for the person and society in general, and in which way – when I say dampening down – it can be best made harmonious with the whole, with the all-over context.

Again, if you get one aspect which possibly, as a result of the person's character, physique or whatever, is slightly more prominent than the others, it should be kept under control so that you don't get any imbalance.

You want to advance things as a whole, reasonably, keeping in step with each other, because you know, as they say, "you can have too much of a good thing." That is exactly the point. If a person finds a degree of spiritual stimulus shall we say, from visiting a place, hearing a particular piece of music, recitation, sound – they may try to enhance that effect by visiting that place more often, listening to that music or that text or whatever it is, more. What they absorb from that will be quite a lot, so that the possibility is that that area can get pushed up to the detriment of the less exciting run-of-the-mill things, so that a person says, "Ooh, I'll listen to that more."

It's a human characteristic, there's nothing terrible about it – it's nothing to be worried about, because the function of the teacher is to look and see and think and then say or do, provoke or precipitate, push or pull, stimulate or damp down. The teacher does not give a spirituality to a person. It is beyond his capacity, ability, function, and certainly, normally beyond his desire to do so. *What he does and should do is to recognize the existence or absence of, the strength or weakness of spirituality, and see in which ways the Tradition can best stimulate this, and in which area.*

No person's being is exactly the same. No person's being remains the same. The time factor comes in. If a person is involved with a use-

ful activity within the Tradition, we do not use terms like "too late" or
"too early." Trains can be too late; trains are never too early, but things
can be too early. If you look at the natural progression of things — what
happens? A flower comes up too early — and the frost — swoosh! — can
get it — right. How do plants learn? A daffodil bulb is hardly one's idea
of the greatest intellect in the world, but it knows the right time. It
doesn't come up in the middle of January because it gets zapped in fifteen minutes. So how are we measuring it? — "That's just a damned
bulb!" Yes, but it's in tune, because it has to be, because it won't survive if it isn't in tune. "Oh, I think I'll shove my head up and have a look
around" — Good luck, Jack. Hundreds of thousands of millions of
generations of daffodil bulbs have learnt — right.

Man has intellect, he has freedom of choice. That's why he does
the damn fool things which he does. It's called freedom. Now I believe
implicitly in freedom, but I mean, personally, I don't have freedom,
which is funny, or may be considered to be funny. You say, "Well, you
seem to be the big cheese around here and you say you don't have
freedom; well, who does, if you don't?" The answer is that it's true, I
have less freedom than any of you. For the simple reason that I am who
I am, and what I am. I should know better than to make a charlie of
myself — you can all go out and make charlies of yourselves, and people
will say, "Oh well, that's the way he is." If I do it, then people are aghast,
horrified, and generally sort of panic-stricken.

Why I don't have freedom is this: I don't have the freedom of indulgence in the sense that if I see somebody who is more or less under
my thralldom, or whatever it's referred to these days, I cannot let them
make a complete fool of themselves in areas in which I have any possibility of intervention. I cannot let my attention wander, "Oh dammit,
I didn't notice that — the fool has done it again, I'd better do something" — no, because this becomes a hit-and-miss. If I happen to be
watching that fool at the time, what about that other fool over there?

So what I have to do is to scan all the time and measure what's going
on. I am responsible — not for them making a fool of themselves — but
I am responsible if I notice that they're likely to make a fool of themselves, and I don't do anything about it when I could do something about
it. Therefore my hands are tied. I have to do something about it.

Why don't you help us all not to make fools of ourselves? Ah, no. Because, take it to one extreme: making a fool of oneself, or developing spiritual aspects, imply a certain amount of volition — there's a certain amount of freedom. But it is easier — very much easier — to make a gigantic fool of oneself rather than to develop oneself enormously — spiritually or in any other way. I'm not saying that one should bear down tremendously on oneself to get tremendously spiritual all the time. You try being tremendously spiritual in a traffic jam when the lights turn green — if there are fifteen people leaning on their horns behind you, you can't say to them, "Brethren, I am being spiritual" — it doesn't work. That is the right thing at the wrong time.

You can be halfway between the absolute charlie — the absolute charlie will stop at the traffic light, get out, remove his back wheels. I think in French they would say he is a "lunatic agrégé" — I mean he will have worked at being so idiotic — but he can be something in between, which is, you know, change gear and move off — that's perfectly all right.

Preoccupation with being constantly spiritual is not a useful thing. *It can engender what I'm always warning against, and that is tension.* A person is going around looking for opportunities for being spiritual and they walk into a lamp-post. This is not useful. They learn — "I should be less spiritual and look where I'm going." Right? Hopefully they'll do it once or maybe twice. If they keep on doing it ... You know there is a weak Hadith, which is one of the Traditions of the Prophet, in which he said that "anybody who is bitten by a snake twice from the same hole is not one of my followers" — which is a very sound thing.

Now of course there are people who are not only bitten successively at the same hole, but take a spade and dig up the snake to make sure that it in fact is a snake. Whereas actually, they should have understood by the time their feet fell off, or something, that in fact it was a snake. "I will examine this to the utmost" — yes, but can you handle the examination, and what can you do with the snake when you've discovered it? Wouldn't it be better, if you have the overwhelming desire to use the spade, to wait until the snake comes out and then bash it, rather than digging it up and saying, "Ooh, it's a snake!" This is not useful.

Now, this is again, extreme. You get people who vary between these extremes, wildly. This is called freedom, individuality, or whatever. You don't necessarily have to aspire to a rigidity of that degree — no. There is a degree of fluctuation, which is perfectly all right, perfectly permissible and not harmful, providing that one knows, reasonably, the limits to this fluctuation. And, if anything, one aspires to a fluctuation towards a spiritual awareness area. I say fluctuation, again, because again this is not the "forcing over" — because that implies, again, tension. When the tension relaxes, it's got to spring back, and it will go further over.

If one appreciates that spirituality is not just a state of being or a state of behaviour, it's not a way of dressing, it is not a performance, it is not a frame of mind — it is all these things. Reacting, feeling, judging by, looking at the terms of reference, being stimulated by one's intention.

"*Joi gul bash, jui khar khar*" — see? Everybody nod wisely? Good. Because that means an age-old sage piece of advice, it's a couplet from Saadi about a rose, and he says, "In the place where a rose is required, a rose is a rose, when a thorn is required it can be thorny" — they are both aspects of the rose, you see?

At a time when one is trying to focus, tune in on, be in harmony with, a spiritual feeling, situation, text, piece of music, recitation or something like that — fine. Relate to it with the terms of reference that you have, focus on it, feel towards it — don't force yourself into that context. When you are in a situation, or in a place, or in a frame of mind or state of being where spirituality is not required, you're not detaching from spirituality, you're not again switching it off — it is always there. It can be latent — which means never really touched, with valid contact with the prevailing situation never really made.

Spirituality is neither a threat, nor is it a promise — it is neither. It is a way of existence within the context. It is always there. After all, if I am using my hand to pick up a glass, am I disregarding my foot or my ear, which is not involved in that operation? The answer is no. I mean, if I pick it up with my foot, that would be a feat which I know is not possible. If I reached down and grasped it with my foot, that would reflect on my ancestry. So therefore it would neither be functional nor useful.

It is not switching off the foot, but what it is doing, is that on a normal action — now I reach out and hold up a glass — now I am holding it. My attention — the attention which relates to the nerves and the signals to this hand, are in action somewhere, telling me exactly how firmly to hold this: I've already judged the weight, size, the amount of flex on my arm — as far as I'm concerned, all the energy is involved in and physi-

cally connected to that. I'm saving energy. The fact that my legs and feet
are relaxed are helping my hand, so that they're not tensed and ready
to carry when I'm holding this glass, because that would be ridiculous
and unnecessary. If I have to remind myself that, just because my hands
are working, these parts of me are also working, then I would have a
problem, apart from the fact that I would be using energy. It is really
very grotesque.

Therefore, if you say, "Oh goodness, I wasn't thinking spiritually"
and you fall to the ground because you are not using your legs to walk
along – you're focusing all your energy and attention to the brain and
therefore you fall over – I think you are bananas.

But you see, the analogy is: there is an extremely complex game –
I only know about four people who can play it. As I mentioned earlier,
it's eight chessboards made out of perspex; and there are eight sets of
pieces on each, and you play a game through the top. And this is very
difficult; this is analogous to the being of the person. These aspects –
*the conscious, the unconscious, the physical, the mental, the spiritual and
so forth – are interleaved with each other.* Looked at from the side point
of view, they may be significantly detached. Looked at from the top-up
point of view, they all relate exactly. So if, on the top chessboard, you
play a move, on level 2, 3, 4, 5, it is impossible; on level 6 that square is
already occupied. Right, you don't make that move. That means that if
that particular square is engaged, the piece which you intended to move
on the top isn't useless, it just is not functional at that moment.

It's the same analogy as the muscles of the arm and the hand which
are being used in this – these other muscles and nerves, in fact, the energy which one would use – are cleared for other uses.

Does that mean then that I should gaze spiritually into this glass,
harnessing the extra energy? No. Because the function is, hopefully, to
hold this, to drink from it, to put it down and then to conserve the extra
energy – use it; a certain amount of it to speak to you; a certain amount
of it to see what's going on everywhere else, and a certain amount to go
to sleep or recharge or whatever.

Therefore spirituality links in on all the levels. It is not attached,
detached, plugged in at a particular time; it is not a constant preoccupation. *If the seed is there; if it is in relation; if it is in harmony; if it is put in
action in the correct context; then it develops harmoniously. It is not an*

aspect of being; it is a part of the being. It is and should be, ideally, the motivation of the being, but not to the exclusion of everything else. This is where you get the overload, the imbalance, the frustration, the complication, the nervousness, the tension and other things: "I should be doing something more useful." Well, do it or shut up.

"I don't like my job, this is a lousy job" — yes, but you know, from that lousy job one eats, or one pays one's gas bill or whatever. One's physical energy — while one is doing a job or an activity which is seemingly unproductive — is at the disposal of who is paying your salary or whatever — but your soul is your own. There is no battle. If it becomes a battle, either change your job if you can, or don't take a job or don't do a job, but do not make the great fight between them: "This is compromise" and so on — no.

Flexibility, harmonious balance — the moment you take up a rigid position, except on questions of principle in which you believe fundamentally, you normally use flexibility. If you believe that spirituality can and does exist, it is capable of developing within the context of the being to produce a constant awareness. This constant awareness is not there in front of your eyes like some sort of esoteric television screen to remind you of the fact it's there — it is a feeling that it is there, that it develops, that there is the capacity to develop. There is a tangible feeling — it is not an abstract concept.

Neither can it be enhanced by any number of extraneous things. As I say, you can put on a robe of a dervish, it doesn't make you into a dervish. A robe, a tasbee, a *kashkul** carried by Dervishes or whatever we use, are aids. They enhance a capacity which one is developing. They are instruments. Their significance is also — or can be and should be — a tangible one, because spirituality is involved in affirmation. A person affirms to themselves that they feel or they believe or they need or they want — or all of these things. There is no harm — in fact it is a useful thing — *to remind oneself of one's intention, and to affirm one's feelings, one's needs and one's beliefs to oneself, because this enhances — this reminds one.* Reminding oneself is not constantly sort of jabbing — it's not an annoyance. It should be — I think it's Salman-i-Farsi who says that *"intention and remembering are not like hailstones; they're like the*

* Beggar bowl

soft patter of rain." So it's not: "Aaargh, I must remember!" — because
that gives you an adrenaline boost, but not much else.

But the gradual and the constant developing also produces a solid
foundation. You can put something together and it looks marvelous on
the outside, but submit it to — not submit it to examination, but submit
it to strain, it'll probably crumble, it'll break. And then everybody looks
around for blame — themselves, somebody else, the context, the world,
God, whatever. There are no tyrants and no victims in this context. One
can punish oneself: it is not a rewarding thing. One can remind oneself
what one is trying to achieve even as vaguely as one can. One says, "Well,
I don't know what I am capable of achieving."

Don't go after sort of black-and-white: "I want to achieve" say,
"awareness, permanent consciousness, feeling" or whatever — it
doesn't matter. Eventually and slowly one narrows down, because —
why? How does one narrow down? By examination and by experience:
"This thing worked;" "That place is such-and-such," "That person is
such-and-such," and then one tends to involve oneself in those valuable
areas more, when one's own time allows. This is not, again, to the exclusion of everything else — "I will only talk to people who are
spiritual" — "I will only visit spiritual places" — "I will only do spiritual
things." This again is an imbalance, because one has not examined and
found wanting certain things and therefore rejected them — no.

One is working in tandem with certain things. There are certain activities one has to do; one doesn't particularly like them, but they're
necessary — so one does them. This is not to the detriment — "Oh, I am
wasting my energy on this." No — because the energy which is valuably
developed with the correct intention is not spent on things which are
not valuable. One has to repeat to oneself the intention, what one's intention is, and follow it up.

It's a very common phenomena in all religions or cultures, to take
a concept or a person or a theory and say, "I would like to be like that
or like that person" or "I would like to think in that way" or "I would
like to be able to be capable of writing that sort of thing" or "doing that
sort of thing" — aspiring to a particular thing. There's nothing wrong in
that, as long as one takes those places, texts, things, people, to be examples of a way of — behaving, thinking, and a way of spirituality. To try
and achieve the same degree of renown of a person is perfectly all right.

But people achieve it also in different ways. There are many ways to achieving anything.

As long as one is quite sure of what one hopes to achieve, and one recognizes the techniques or the instruments or the path which one wants to follow – then you can be sure of one thing – as far as the Tradition is concerned, there is guidance along the road. There is a definite path and it can be followed, it has been followed, and there's no reason why it shouldn't be followed, because there's one very good reason why it should be followed, and that is because it has to be followed. The alternative is – let's say, not in the best interests of our children.

Now that is not an ominous threat and a horrid note to end on – it is that the freedom which a person has to do something valid – for themselves, for their children and others – is attracted and should attract a positive. It is not "a thinking person can only think in this way" – no. Because thinking, again, is a vague area; it presupposes either intellectual ability or something like that – this is a feeling activity. A person measures it, feels it, reactions come in a deeper way.

This is why we have no sort of written examinations and that sort of thing, because again, this would be a conditioned judgment, this would be attempting to measure the intangible with, if you like, tangible means, and it's not possible. It would be time-consuming, and also it would be an end in itself.

Chapter 10

PRECISE AND IMPRECISE THINKING

How imprecision leads man to abdicate his own responsibility for aware-ness; How man's terms of reference must remain within a harmonious context; How imbalanced activities work against one; Worldly and material values; Child's absorption capacity; How it has always been pos-sible to develop harmoniously; How prayer and belief are insufficient by themselves; Necessity of a permanent consciousness; The Tradition as a focus for learning; Communication on sophisticated and unsophisticated levels; How the world is increasingly concerned with itself rather than its place within an overall pattern.

Thinking correctly avoids imprecision. It is relevant, within the Tradition, that the lack of precision in doing things or carrying things out is usually a direct result of a lack of precision in thinking. That's no great sensational discovery, but I find that it is symptomatic of many of the problems which exist today within people as individuals, within families, groups, and society as a whole.

One defines certain terms of reference, and under most cir-cumstances one tries to stay within, and to redefine, these terms of reference. Occasionally one finds that one will act in a more efficient way, based, again, on clear thinking and clear terms of reference, in such a way that we come to a point which cannot really be over-stressed: it brings one into a harmonious way of thinking, which in turn provokes harmonious situations, harmonious activities.

Man is a creature of the universe — and all that that implies. However, in his arrogance, because he is alleged to be a rational, think-ing, intellectual being — as compared, I suppose, to hoi-polloi and other entities in the universe — man defines his own terms of reference in the universe, and if they are outside the harmonious context of the universe in the galaxy, he causes himself trouble, and, in a sense, it can affect both the galactic order and his own development in a negative way. If man exercises and shows this arrogance, it is because he has been either conditioned into, or has conditioned himself into, employing terms of reference that are not only inharmonious, but actually hostile to the context in which he lives, and in which he wishes to develop himself.

He produces every technological circumstance; he tries to produce sociological, political, economic and other circumstances in which he hopes to be able to develop himself and hopefully develop others. All these advantages – educational, sociological, technological – are very laudable, necessary and worthwhile, provided that they do not produce a lopsided situation where these become either totally a means to an end or an end in themselves.

For instance, if he develops a global technological circumstance without reference to what in the old-fashioned terminology would be called a balanced educational, cultural, philosophical and spiritual activity – contemporaneously – then inevitably he runs into problems, as he has run into them now. He has very often used the intellect, intelligence, discrimination and other things which have been developed throughout civilization in a lopsided way. Too much emphasis has been placed on one aspect of development, and little importance has been placed on other aspects – very often because they have no tangible value – that is to say, they don't figure on a balance-sheet, in election results, in examination results, in social prominence – therefore they are considered as possibly not very important.

In specific educational and cultural areas – as I say, in the old-fashioned way – education begins in the home: children emulate their parents, they follow their parents' example. Culturally, a child growing up, a person in a cultural situation, will absorb and use the culture in which he is brought up. If it is a valuable culture, if it is harmonious, instructive, and encouraging – he will accept it and he will follow it.

In the area of what one might call broadly the spiritual, man either decides or has decided that this is everybody's own problem, everybody's own privilege to accept or to differ – or else they hand over their spiritual well-being to organizations – organized religion. Organized religion is a perfectly laudable and reasonable thing; everybody should have a belief and be guided by the precepts of that belief. However, the function of an organized religion is to assist in a social and cultural as well as in an educational way, and to be a source of comfort, help and guidance, spiritual and otherwise – but it does not replace the individual's responsibility towards himself.

A person can and should grow up in the context of a religion, whatever religion it may be, and this religion is the basis for the person's onward development. Nobody can do this development for you – whether it be the local vicar, bishop, archbishop, cardinal, rabbi, imam, sheikh, whatever – they can be a symbol for a particular religion. Hopefully they will be men of wisdom, humility, charity, modesty – and they will be there to advise or encourage, give comfort and generally act in a positive way. However, if we talk of what, if you like, is beyond religion – that doesn't mean outside the context of religious belief, religious expression or religious feeling – it is where the responsibility of the person to aim for, and hopefully achieve, a higher consciousness comes in. Nobody can do it for you.

Man in his arrogance has explained away or tried to scientifically describe so-called phenomena. Sometimes it's because they are agnostics, or people who say that "If I can't see it, measure it, weigh it, I won't accept it or believe it." Sometimes it is because they wish for control, and they think, "Right, if we can explain phenomena on some sort of a scientific basis, we can recreate this phenomena, therefore people can be detached from some sort of spiritual belief and they will believe in us rationalists, scientists," whatever it is.

Man is arrogant and greedy and he has another characteristic, which is laziness. Because he is lazy he tends to abdicate his responsibility towards himself and hand it over to people who will represent him or who will take the burden of responsibility off his shoulders. Man throughout civilization has given away great chunks of his own responsibility towards himself.

You have various professions: you have doctors, lawyers, you have judges, you have peacekeepers, you have members of Parliament – now I'm not suggesting that every person become his own doctor, his own lawyer and everything else, because throughout history a certain responsibility has been given to people because they were knowledgeable, trained, necessary, and because their activity was harmonious within the context of society. A doctor, certainly with the help of science and other knowledges, heals the sick – fine. A lawyer arbitrates, sorts out problems, and negotiates. A judge hears the evidence and he makes the decisions. A policeman keeps an eye on things – maintains the rule of law. A soldier defends the community and attacks the enemy of that particular society.

If man is not expected to heal himself, sue people, pursue the transgressor, judge, keep peace, and do all these functions – if he is not expected to do all these, then fine. He can give responsibility away: he gives this responsibility freely in elections to his elected Borough Councillor or member of Parliament, and he hopes that this person he has elected will represent him in the fullest sense. The election of a representative to a council is almost as old as man himself; it is functional and it is useful. In a country, say, of fifty million people, it should not be necessary for all those fifty million people to meet together in one place and talk about it before any laws can be passed, the very logistics are absolutely appalling. So therefore each area, constituency or whatever elects a representative and they go to Parliament with the mandate from their electors to represent them: to be their voice. The electorate hopes that this man will have their best interest at heart, and will represent them. The responsibility is upon that man to do so.

If he is idle, greedy, shiftless, incompetent, idiotic or anything else, he will do a bad job, the people will be ill-represented and at the next election they may throw him out and put somebody else in. Fine. The damage is probably not very great.

If a people agree that their consciences or their souls, or responsibility for their consciences or their souls will be handed over lock, stock and barrel in some curious way to a clergy – and when I say clergy I mean whatever denomination or whatever religion – and very often too, a person may very well be in that job for life – firstly, this area is open to abuse; secondly, I think that it saps the intention of the individual. This may be a sweeping statement but I think there is adequate proof to show it.

In the area of the organization of a church, the terms of reference are, and should be, very clear. The function of a church – apart from christening, burying, and all the other things – is to be an advisory body, and to try and work harmoniously within the system and to offer the comfort and the haven and security which people need. However it cannot and should not be expected either to dominate, or to take on the responsibility of looking after people's souls. People's souls are their own. What they do with them, you might say, is their own problem.

It may be their own problem, but you can't just dismiss it like that, and say, "Go off and find your own salvation" or "Your soul is your own; as is your responsibility to develop harmoniously, in a cosmic sense" — and I'm not talking about flying saucers and that sort of rubbish when I talk about the cosmos — your responsibility is your own. The next question of course is: "I accept that it is, so what do I do about it?" Regarding the bishop, the archbishop, the rabbi, mullah, the imam, or whatever it is — "Are you going to take the responsibility of telling me exactly what to do, so that I can then say, 'Oh, I did that, and it was a mistake, but so-and-so told me to do it, therefore I'm not responsible; he's responsible.'?"

What you must have is recognition of the fact that there are, and always have been, possibilities for the harmonious development of man within the context of his normal social, economic, political, or educational development. Being in the world but not of the world.

A person can go to a religious leader or any religious man, pour out his troubles and ask what he should do, and so often the answer is "believe" or "pray." Both these activities are to be recommended and they're very laudable — however there are other questions which, without over-intellectualizing, come from that: to whom or how to pray, and in what or in whom to believe? Supposing one says, "All right, I was brought up in a particular religious system, and the method of prayer and to whom to pray is very clear to me" — fine. In the Tradition, we do not accept that that alone, or rather those two factors, essential as they may be — are enough. *We hold that the permanent consciousness, which is one of the things that one aims for in the Tradition — permanent, deep and harmonious consciousness — is an absolute necessity.* How one arrives at this, or how one aspires to arrive at it, again, in the Tradition, is very clearly laid out. *I would stress again that harmonious development is the whole secret.*

The imposition of an arrogant alien impulse, which man brings to the scheme of things, throws things out of kilter. You would not consciously drop a handful of sand into a delicate watch mechanism — people say, "Of course I wouldn't do a thing like that" — but man does it consistently. While an oyster can produce a pearl from a grain of sand, society and mankind cannot produce millions and millions of pearls as a result of all the sand which they throw consistently and in a dedicated fashion into what could be and should be a harmonious humanity.

If any false individual entity, planet, or creature introduces something alien into a harmonious system, either the system absorbs it and controls it, as in the case of the oyster – the oyster coats the grain of sand until it is no longer hurtful and dangerous – or society itself becomes polluted by this, for this alien point of view or term of reference moves into the new context and becomes a term of reference.

In a harmonious society, extraneous influences or terms of reference, are not automatically and by definition negative and destructive. I use the word "alien" because it implies something hostile and aggressive, something which possibly wants to take over, or manifests itself in a disproportionate way.

Again, very often in his arrogance or his laziness, man allows this alien point of reference, train of thought, to obscure what should be *the true focus of his attention, which is a harmonious relationship with everything else around him within the cosmos.* Man declares a Unilateral Declaration of Independence, because he is rational, intelligent and intellectual, because he is created in "God's own image." Well, if he is – if he is so marvelous, which is what he says he is, why does he consistently – in an individual, family, group, country, or world context – not only make a mess of things over and over again, following the same pattern based on stupidity, greed, laziness – while at the same time he is selling short or adopting a scornful attitude to things which are beyond his understanding, which he hasn't been able to describe, capture, or control?

I think here you have one of the explanations why he does this. Certain phenomena, which might be called psychic phenomena, are beyond man's control in the sense that he cannot provoke these – he cannot switch them on or switch them off. He can't sell them to people, and, more difficult to accept, he can't buy them. He automatically considers what he can't buy and what he can't control to be a menace to his power mania or his money. In regard to the existence or the possibility of experiencing these phenomena – the fact that he considers them as a possible menace, is, I think, evidence of his own arrogance and stupidity.

You might say that is a sweeping statement: not every body thinks so—no. Not everybody considers that to be the case, but a significant proportion of what unfortunately have become the attitude-making or terms of reference-making bodies throughout the world have declared some of these phenomena or experiences or terms of reference to be anathema—from their political, economic, social or other points of view.

And man allows them to be declared anathema. Man allows them to be sold short, sneered at, laughed at and generally despised. And I personally view this with a considerable amount of alarm and a great amount of sorrow.

For instance when you hear two or three people talking, and they say, "Well, you know I think such-and-such a thing might happen" or "Such-and-such a thing is happening—my old granny thinks this or feels that or said she felt it in her bones that this was going to happen" and you get the sort of apologetic laugh: "Well, you know what she's like …" Yes, I know exactly what she's like, and I sympathize with her. This sneering, leering attitude towards some, by their measurements, gaga person, who is almost certainly more in tune with the natural scheme of things—such a sneering and leering attitude is an indictment. All right, now when I say the person gives an "apologetic" laugh, it is because he is almost certainly afraid of saying, "This is what my old granny thinks and I think the same"—because they're either going to tap their foreheads and turn away, or, and this is the striking thing—even worse, the fellow who says that is using the apologetic laugh or that kind of attitude because he is afraid that other people will say, "Yes, we know exactly what you mean and we feel the same"—and they will all be left saying, "What do we do now?"

I find it a terrible indictment that a person, or two or three people, cannot say things which they feel or which they think. Very often, they use a third person, it's a classic thing: somebody goes into a pawnbroker and says, "My friend has asked me to pawn this watch." The pawnbroker knows perfectly well it's the fellow's own watch, because he's continually pulling his sleeve down to conceal the fact—okay, that's a delicate area, it is embarrassing—but using the third person is also very often to avoid saying that in fact, "I think that this, that and the other thing is happening." "I heard a chap in the train today and he said I think the world is coming to an end," and everybody else says, "He must be a lunatic," so the fellow thinks to himself, "Well thank goodness I didn't say that I was the one who thought the world was going to come to an end."

So people use this. But they also use it to test out the water; if they get a little bit of feedback, maybe on the way out of the pub in the car-park, one of the fellows says, "Well, that was interesting, Jones, what you said about your old granny, because yes, grannies are like that, but you know, I remember when I was a child ..." or something like that, and this will very often come out. A lot more people think that there is another harmony, and are unable to find either the contacts or the words to describe it, or a context within which it can be — "discussed" I suppose is the word — although it is not necessary to discuss or debate an experience which does not have precise terms of reference in the West.

You lump together whole things and you call them feelings. Well, that's fine, there's no problem there, but it is imprecise. Because if you say you have a feeling of discomfort in your knee — you can say, "Well, actually that is not a feeling, that is an actual pain" — so that there is an actual technical word for that particular feeling. If you say, for instance, "I had a feeling" — "I went to such-and-such a place and I had a feeling that something was wrong" or "I had a feeling that things were not quite right" — you're getting into an area of possible lack of precision. One could argue that, yes, that was all it was; it was a feeling — you can't say it was an anguish, or a pain, or a cold or it was hot or nervous-making or agitating — people say, "It was a sort of feeling." Well in this area it's possible to get away with saying, "There was a slight feeling in the air" or something — that's all right. Possibly, if there is no necessity for precision, then one can let it go at that.

However, *in the Tradition we aim for as much precision as possible, and this precision and the use of such precision, has to be learned.* It's not a thing in which you're given a book, a sort of A to Z, look up "feel-ings" and then it explains everything — no. Because that again would have been somebody else doing your work for you. Human nature, the human frame, the human system, the human being is such, that, even though the basic building bricks are there, and the foundation is there — a person does not inherit the ability to speak a language.

Genetically, racially, there are certain abilities – for instance if you take a simple example in eastern languages which we use – in Arabic, there is a letter *"ain"* which is called a glottal stop. Strangely enough, it is a contortion of the larynx. Some people are incapable of making that sound, yet Arab-speaking children, babies from Arab-speaking stock, are born with a certain laryngeal capacity, which is an ability to form that without great effort. That is a racial, genetic, characteristic – and it's all very interesting. Does this mean to say that people who are brought up with more intimate contact with the Tradition can benefit from it more, or have some genetic ability which is greater than others? The answer by and large is no.

Just as a child learns a language, a person can learn an activity. A baby is born without a language. He usually learns the language of the family in which he's brought up, by hearing, by mimicry, by experiment, and by being taught how to pronounce correctly, how to expand his vocabulary. If a child is brought up in a poor village in very limited circumstances, among peasants where the vocabulary is not particularly rich – that child is not saddled with the limited vocabulary of his or her parents. If the child goes to school, it is taught how to expand and exercise its vocabulary, how to exercise its language. This is a thing which is learned. So, in the Tradition, techniques of exercising the basic capacity are learned, and they are exercised, and they are used consciously and unconsciously, following a very precise pattern.

We have words, phrases, technical terms, to explain certain feelings; and they are not confused with physical technical terms – but they are very precise, so that if one is discussing a particular experience with another person who is familiar with these technical terms and one uses the proper technical term, if the other person has experienced it, this will immediately strike a chord with the other person, and they will say, "Right, yes, okay" – therefore the area of discussion or debate is taken away: "Will you describe exactly what the feeling was? Did you feel hot, cold, nervous, frightened, happy, drunk, sober, light-headed, dopey, heavy, lopsided or what?" No.

The word describing the experience is so precise – it is not just that the other person nods wisely because they've read or learned that term of reference or precise term and they know what it's supposed to mean – it strikes also a deeper chord within them, because this term of reference has a sonority value – the sound of it – because we aim after all to use all the senses when we're talking, when we're communicating. It's not just the famous thought transfer, it can be learned. It's useful functionally, and it is especially useful if a lot of people are talking and there's a great hubbub and two people want to communicate – they don't have to shout at each other. Or if they want to communicate above the background of the glug-glugging of other people's brains and the clicking and thundering of thought. No, communication takes place on various what are called sophisticated levels, but they're not really all that sophisticated. They are sophisticated because they're supposed to be in a rarified area, and they are lumped together with all sorts of esotericism and what-have-you, which I suppose is very rewarding and fascinating if one is into the generalization of esotericism, rather than into precision – but I happen to believe more in precision, in precise thinking, which means shearing-off the wooly extrapolations of so-called intellectual exercise.

Some intellectuals produce awesome riddles and compound the esoteric riddle that what noise, say, do sabre-toothed tigers colliding in the dark make? And the answer is of course that they don't make any noise, because if it's a sabre-tooth tiger, well you've had it. And you've got two around, and it's in the dark – you've had it doubly. So the propounding of these esoteric questions have consumed lifetimes and tomes, and they're very workmanlike jobs of work if one has the time and the inclination to plough through screeds and volumes and try and arrive at some coherent, intelligent, harmonious discipline which can be followed in a world which is increasingly concerned with itself – rather than its place in a cosmic pattern.

If man decides, which he does and has, that he is the greatest thing since sliced bread or whatever – then he is in danger of worshipping his own product to the exclusion of everything else. If you are a Ford motor car salesman, it is more than your job is worth to knock your product and say, "This is a lousy car, I would go down the road and buy a Jaguar" or something like that. So you go about mouthing the fact that the Ford motor car is the greatest thing on earth – fine. If you believe it, fine. If you don't believe it, at least leave that fable behind when you leave that office at night and drive home in your Jaguar.

There is no need for compromise – if you want to become the famous company man who believes that the sun rises and sets on Ford – fine. You'll probably end up as a millionaire with ulcers and all the other things which come along with it – but if you believe that it is possible to develop harmoniously, being in the world and not of the world – without compromising, without becoming a martyr to your belief, without finding it necessary to go up on the mountain-side and call in a loud voice to Humanity – if you believe that these things can be done, then for evidence of this, all you have to do is look at the structure of the cosmos and see that everything follows a pattern.

As I have said before, I think that man's esteem of his intellect, intelligence, terms of reference and so forth causes him to be the rebellious element in the cosmos. He gets up in the morning and has authority – either social, economic, or political – and possibly as a result of the fact that he either has a hangover or his feet hurt or something – as an individual, he is capable of starting a war, a world war, a localized war or whatever, with unimaginable results to himself, to his family, to his society, to his culture, and to his world.

Right. He has independence. He has liberty. Beyond a certain point liberty becomes license. His independence can be hostile arrogance, "I'm all right, Jack." Imagine for a moment what would have happened if the vegetable or animal kingdom decided also that they were inheritors of independence and liberty. Suppose cabbages and lettuces decided to grow downwards? Suppose birds ran about kicking people – that's independence? For instance, how many hundreds and thousands of generations of guinea hens have there been? Supposing an actual guinea hen of today woke up and said, "I am the eight hundred and seventy thousand millionth guinea hen; ergo, I am the inheritor of eight hundred and seventy thousand million generations of development – I will logically then be the size of a cart-horse, and I will go over there and kick that policeman or traffic warden!" It would cause a certain amount of turmoil and confusion, if each creature proportionately decided to do this. You'd have the bird life going around kicking traffic wardens, you'd have lettuces showing their independence by growing downwards, you'd have tigers and lions rushing up mountains and leaping off flapping their legs – because why shouldn't they fly for a change? Supposing, at the end of its orbit, a planet decides, "I don't think I'll adhere to this apogee and perigee business" — which is dictated by magnetic fields — "I think I'll just turn myself round and I'll go the other way." That is the end of your actual planet, and a lot of other planets who happen to be the innocent victims of this planet's so-called independence or freedom of choice.

Well fortunately for this planet, other planets which are significantly bigger than this imperceptible dot, do not have freedom of choice, they turn and they move according to pre-determined laws. You might say, "Well, they don't have much choice — who are we to say?" We say we have choice, we have freedom of choice, so therefore we can screw everything up, and this is Democracy, freedom, liberty and everything else. "Those old planets wandering about and speeding about and that sort of thing, they don't have freedom of choice" — how do you know?

It is arrogant to suppose that they have no freedom of choice. Suppose they have freedom of choice and they have decided for their own well-being and for the well-being of other planetary bodies, that they will adhere to a self-imposed discipline? If this planet decided to unilaterally shift its axis, there wouldn't be very much damage to the solar system, but there would be a very significant damage to the Earth. Humanity should be damned grateful that this planet has not decided, as a planet, to shift its axis a bit — or to go into another orbit nearer the sun, maybe to rid itself of a lot of arrogant people strutting around saying that they are the greatest thing in creation.

They don't know. You have a certain proportion of loonies squinting through telescopes, and because they can't see the delights of civilization like high-rise buildings and spaghetti junctions, they think there is no life anywhere else. I am not saying that life is little green men, but life is certainly not spaghetti junctions all over the place. So the terms of reference which are used, fuel the arrogance which man shows to his environment, to his world, and to the galaxy in which he lives.

For goodness sake, apart from babbling and raving, what has all this got to do with precision? Very simply that the moment precise terms of reference are either deliberately obscured or shoved under the carpet, or dropped behind a convenient hedge so that they won't be embarrassing; the moment people cease to use correct, precise terms of reference, you get an enormous uncalled for, unnecessary, and deleterious flexibility within the fabric of society.

If that's an indigestible phrase: what it comes down to is that humanity is rapidly getting itself up a creek without a paddle. And then they flail around and don't realize, again in their arrogance, that there is a paddle. They have allowed the leaders, statesmen, politicians, and other people with vested interests, to tell them what the paddles are or what paddles they should use. They have, if you like, "educated" people out of using their own feelings or precise terms of reference to say: "No that's not the right paddle" – "Oh yes it is, because all paddles are painted red and therefore that's a paddle" – a paddle is a paddle is a paddle – no way. Again, you do not have everybody having hundreds of different paddles of all different colours just because they happen to like that colour – that again would be a recipe for chaos. But it is not at all necessary that one source of knowledge, technique or whatever should decide and tell you which paddle one uses.

Various things are agreed upon as being useful, beneficial to mankind, society and the cosmos, by general consent, based on knowledge, examination, experience and evaluation. You have a thing which, by common consent, is considered necessary and essential: for instance, a compass. By almost universal consent, a compass is accepted as being a useful and a valuable thing. The basic compass was there, it was modified, adapted for use in different circumstances; but still, the basic quality, value, capacity, and nature of the compass has been guarded.

Take a compass which points towards a certain point – you could not technically make a thing in the same form out of sago and expect it to perform the same function. You could put up an enormous poster with an arrow pointing to this saying "The World's First Sago Compass" but it wouldn't work – and those who then paddled out from the pool of London or whatever with a sago compass, would find that it was a disappointing experience. The vested interest in this case would be the manufacturer of the sago compass, whose hope would be that the people would get far enough away and get lost, and not come back saying, "Your infernal compass didn't work" and beat the tar out of them. They are working on the assumption that there are no comebacks. The moment they see somebody staggering up the path, pulped to pieces, carrying a sago compass which has dissolved in sea-water, heat, etc. — they will shut up shop. But they are clever enough, either to move shop so that, in the event that the fellow does make it back there'll be no comeback; or hopefully they'll vanish over the horizon, and anyway the world is flat, so there they go.

These may be ridiculous assumptions, but a certain segment of society fosters the sago compass theory. A compass is a compass is a compass. "The fact that it's sago doesn't matter because we've made a great breakthrough, and anyway sago is good for you." — "But I don't want sago, I want a compass." — "Well, just try the sago first, and you know, things will become easier." They will become easier, because since you know or fear or think that the compass is sago, you don't go anywhere, you stay where you are, and you end up perhaps eating the sago, and even getting to like the sago, but it is not replacing the compass which is supposed to get you from A to B.

You do not get totally pessimistic about everybody, and you're not totally optimistic, but you certainly don't believe that there is anything to be achieved without precise effort. "Oh, I think I'll just wander about until somebody just tells me which way is North" — that's fine, but when somebody tells you which way is North and they point you the right way — firstly, and this is not meant to be an unkindness to those people who are so afflicted — if that person happens to be cross-eyed, you may have a problem. If however, you have every reason to believe that the person has a pretty good idea of which way is North, then the responsibility is on you to take advantage of further signposts along the way, and those signposts do exist, and they are precise — if it is a signpost.

If you go up to a thing, which is painted on a tree, and it says, "This may go North or it may go South or North by Southeast or Good Luck, Jack" — then that is not a signpost. It may have a sign on top of it saying, "This is a signpost" but if it is not precise enough, then you are on the wrong track. You can't say, "Ah, I followed it, it said it is a signpost." You have a certain amount of discrimination — it has nothing to do with intelligence. Therefore you can't put the blame on your lack of activity or you are confusing the tree for the signpost.

Precise thinking, not tensed up — not anxiety-thinking — but precise, calm, dedicated, harmonious thinking produces similar results. This is inevitable in a harmonious context. If man introduces an inharmonious element into a natural context, this is a recipe for disaster. Nobody has ever been into a forest, a jungle, a tropical area, where they have seen a colour or flower which has been of an obnoxious colour, because flowers, for instance, are not dyed by aniline dye. The dyes there are natural. If there is an inharmonious colour in a tropical environment — usually, a shocking colour, a striking colour — it's probably either a venomous thing, which is a warning light; or it's a flap which has fallen off a Boeing 707 or something. It's something which has been introduced into the situation, it has not grown up in harmony with the situation.

The recipe is: harmonious activity and thought, harmonizing with the correct context, produces a harmonious result.

Chapter 11

ENSURING CONTINUITY IN THE TEACHING

Importance of continuity to ensure increasing participation by future generations; Authenticity of experienced instances to ensure continuity of the spoken word; First-person communication; Importance of copyist in transmission; Force of energy in texts and objects.

By definition, continuity in a teaching or in history keeps things together and on a straight line. If you have continuity, especially in a teaching, each successive generation benefits to a greater extent from the activities of the generation before, in that they have hopefully absorbed energy, knowledge and teaching from something like the Tradition, and have passed it on in the form of knowledge, behaviour, contact and teaching to their children.

It becomes all the more valuable when continuity, as in the Tradition, is based on two main factors: one factor being incontrovertible, unedited, uninterpreted books. We have what has come down to us — the writings of the various great masters which have been set down and which have come down to us unaltered through the centuries because they were never the monopoly of a very small clique who kept these books and gave out pieces of information or interpretation as it suited them.

The contents of these writings were very carefully guarded within the Tradition; they were known to a relatively large number of people, so any change of misinterpretation which might occur as a result of a translation or a bad copy or something like that could very quickly be corrected. With any of the great teachers — Jami, Hafiz, Rumi, Saadi, Ibn Arabi, Salman-i-Farsi — there were at any one moment at least four hundred people extant who knew each book absolutely by heart — they could recite it at any moment — so they were the constant, what we call the "pool" to which any translation, any interpretation, any aspect, was submitted and approved.

If it was an area for which there was any doubt in interpretation, especially when it came to a translation – that translation was submitted for approval and there was a majority decision as to the translation or the interpretation of that phrase. If it didn't match up, then it wasn't permitted to be circulated – by circulated, I mean recommended for reading or circulation. One cannot and does not have access to every translation or every interpretation of every book which has ever been written about us in order to correct it, because there are free presses all over the world, they can print all sorts of things, they can make all sorts of wild interpretations – it does make things complicated sometimes – but, by and large, the majority of the books which come out have some useful basis.

The second very valuable aspect of continuity is the oral, the vocal, the sound continuity. This form of continuity is in the form of the spoken word, that is, people who know these various books, people who know the languages involved, and people who can not only just recite them, but explain them as they have heard them being explained. Again, it becomes the first person: "I heard so-and-so explain that ... If somebody says, "I was present when Jami or Rumi said such-and-such a thing, or gave such an answer to a particular question," that is considered to be an authoritative quotation.

If it becomes the soup of the soup: "I heard somebody who was driving a taxi at the time say that I think so-an-so said to somebody ..." – this is not considered to be correct, and therefore it's rejected. It may go into sort of folklore or an apocryphal type of thing, but it's not the "hard" interpretation, the correct interpretation. Throughout history teachers have always been careful – because they have had to be – to make sure that any quotation or explanation or commentary which they give on the work of a past teacher has to be not just party line, but completely authentic – and it has to be in the spirit of the intention of the original author. Word-for-word is not always the right way to do it – after all, circumstances, situations, change – when the rigid word-for-word application is too rigid, and under political, social and other pressures, the technique can break, or break the people it's being applied to.

So the flexibility comes in here. A person who is interpreting or commenting has to know without any shadow of a doubt what the spirit and what the intention was of the author behind that phrase.

Perhaps it was directed to a particular country or a particular group of people or a particular age group or something, therefore it wouldn't necessarily apply word-for-word, chapter-and-verse, in the present circumstances. But if one can reel back and find out exactly what the intention was behind it, and then explain it on the basis of that intention, then one doesn't go far wrong.

In the Tradition, we do rely and have relied heavily upon this first-person communication. We talk about the various "lines" of the teaching. The situation usually is that a teacher will impart aspects of the teaching to other people verbally and by contact, when such aspects have to be carried on into future generations. All this—everything which he says when he teaches—has to be intimately capable of being compared with the actual texts which exist—because any variation between the two causes confusion.

It's a very human thing—a person might hear me talking about something, and subsequently read Rumi or somebody like that, and find that there seems to be a variation in interpretation or meaning. This of course can cause a certain amount of confusion: "Do I challenge it or do I accept it, or which horse do I ride in this circumstance?" As far as I'm concerned I don't think anybody would find any variation, but as I've said before, if there's any significant variation; then always, as far as I or anybody else is concerned, the existent authoritative texts are always the privileged ones: that is to say, everything is to be compared to them. If it is not correct according to the text—not necessarily textually, but in the spirit and the intention—then the text must be considered more authentic.

The importance of maintaining the purity of the texts is so overwhelming that there are existent, at any one time, several copies of any significant text—whether it's, as I say, Rumi, Hafiz, Saadi, Jami, Ibn Arabi or anybody else. And these texts, which are based on the original manuscripts—the original facsimile volumes—are all recognized, because they're all in recognizable handwriting. No two people write in the same way. In the case of the so-called "accepted" copyists—the people who copy the manuscripts—their handwriting is known, so therefore any change or sort of washing out and writing in something else would be immediately identifiable.

At any given moment, there are at least forty copies written by contemporary copyists based on the original manuscript, and those manuscripts are always in safe hands and they can always be compared — because they are of such significant value that there is no possibility that they could be changed around, swapped around, or quoted out of context. The value of a document is not only in what it says, it is the amount of energy and intention which has been put into it by the writer and also by the copyist. There are certain very significant requirements and regulations for a person who is copying a particular manuscript. When he is copying, he must be in a very special state of relationship with the writer — he must be "tuned in" with him, so that any variation in the writing from the original manuscript will signal to him something in the writing, and he'll copy it, so that if, in the calligraphic sweep of the writing, a line is deeper or thicker than usual, he will copy it exactly — it's the equivalent of underlining it or writing it in red, or something like that.

I have seen, for instance, one very good example of this, published at enormous expense by a university in Europe in 1951. It is a text by Ibn al-Arabi, and it is printed in Arabic. It is from a contemporary copy of one of his writings — and it has lost about thirty percent, because with printed words and letters, you can't get the complete original. The man who copied it, when he saw the *alif* or the *bey*, he just put the a or the b — the fact that this was thicker or that was thinner didn't mean anything to him. He just copied it off the manuscript onto the typewriter. Textually, it's perfectly correct, but the emphasis of various things — for instance, one thing used by calligraphers is: when you're writing a phrase or word which is descriptive but not very important, you use thinner ink — it's slightly lighter as distinct from the dark black — you get a slightly sepia tone. You might say, "Well, why did he write it at all? Why didn't he just leave it out?" — because it's what is called in English, a "throwaway" — you don't have to read it, but it just maybe connects one phrase or idea with another.

How can you do that when you're printing a text? The answer is you can't. You put it into parenthesis, which doesn't mean anything. So, while textually, this book — which is fifteen hundred pages long — was absolutely correct, reading it from our point of view means that it didn't mean so much, because the emphatic style which he used was lost because it was like reading a newspaper. It was very interesting, fascinating, correct terminologically and everything like that — but lifeless.

Another example was a very complete publication which was written in 1040 in Teheran. There was a book which was called the *Aflari - Maulana*, the thoughts, the ideas of Rumi. It was part of a notebook of his that he wrote — various ideas and thoughts and that sort of thing. Half of it was in Arabic, half was in Dari — which is Afghan Persian — and it was incorrect. Textually, again, it was perfectly good but it didn't make sense because the colloquialisms which he has used were nuances: they weren't open to interpretation, because he wrote very well — and for instance, when he used a colloquial word, it didn't mean to say he couldn't think of anything else to say, he did it deliberately, because he was a Balkhi, which is northern Afghanistan, and they have a colloquial style of language.

A commentator or translator normally reads a book innumerable times first, to get an idea of the style, the vocabulary, the punctuation, the emphasis and all that sort of thing — and only then does he start translating. If, for instance, he is reading from a very flowery ecclesiastical text and the man has written down: "And it came to pass that he came upon them, and he saith unto them: Buzz off!" — at that point, normally a translator would stop, and he would think: If a man's normal style is the first person — and suddenly he says "shove off" or something, this may not be a very deep philosophical thing, but it indicates something. What does it indicate? It indicates that in normal terms — in reasonable and polite conversation — one doesn't say to people: "Buzz off!"

So therefore if you say "Buzz off" it giveth you an idea to whom he saith that — that they are worthy of buzzing off. If they had been the Lords Spiritual, he could have said: "Getteth thee hence" or whatever they say. So therefore, without saying in parentheses "they, the horrid plebes who were surrounding him closely" — in just one sentence, it shows why he used that particular pejorative phrase.

By definition, the translator and everybody in the world, almost, knows that Rumi was a Balkhi. He was born speaking Dari as his mother language, so when he writes a phrase — he goes, for instance, from

Arabic into perfectly correct archaic Persian; and for instance — it's a literal translation, a Dari phrase — in the summer it's very hot in Maazar-i-Sharif so people sleep on the roof — and he says: "One night I was lying awake on my roof looking at the canopy of stars, and admiring" — and he names various constellations — and then he says "My reverie was disturbed by the sound of somebody scrabbling at the wall. On observing that it was a burglar, I rose from my mattress and, as his head appeared over the parapet, kicked him in the chops" — right. Now this is perfectly understandable; *"Da ruhish laghat zadam"* is the exact phrase, which means, "I kicked him in the chops."

Why use that? Well, it shows that the fellow was a burglar, the reaction to a burglar was to kick him in the face — perfectly laudable — you don't negotiate with a burglar, phone the police, scream — you kick him in the chops, which is exactly what he did. Now that shows what the situation was, and what the man deserved, he got — and finish. And then he goes on with his explanation and the comments about the heavenly beauties, and so forth and so on.

The Irani version had him rising — what was the phrase — "rising startled yet unafraid, dealing with the intruder in a fashion dictated by the spiritual values of his state" or something like that — and when you're reading through that, everybody of course who knew — I mean most Afghans know chapter and verse Rumi — and they're all waiting for the payoff when he gets up and kicks the fellow in the chops; and then they're taken onto this sentimentally beauteous wave of something "and my situation thus ameliorated" — by kicking the fellow in the chops — "I then returned to my study of the stars." Well, he didn't say anything like that: his state was not ameliorated by kicking the fellow in the chops — the fellow got the punishment for shinning up and trying to rob this poor old fellow, and this sort of flight of fancy is ridiculous.

Now why does one dwell at such great length on this? Because there's a very familiar pattern here. From: "I got up from lying down, kicked him in the chops, then went back to studying the stars" — right, end of lesson — it becomes, "I then got up, dealt with him in a manner befitting his state, and having ameliorated my condition, returned to my concentration" — right. Fine. That's Stage 1.

Stage 2 is: Somebody will then take that and expand it. You can see it. I've seen it done. They say, "Hmm, I dealt with him in a manner according to his state" — the only "state" he had was shinning up his drainpipe. But "his state, which, unfortunate wretch, had come upon him because of deprivation" or "he was born under an unlucky star" — goodness knows what — and "they having attended to him in a manner befitting" — which means anything — "he pulled him up, gave him a glass of champagne, gave him a cup of tea," whatever, then, "having restored my equilibrium" and so forth, "I returned to my bed."

Okay. Supposing now you take it — and this is not to a ridiculous degree — you leave in "I kicked him in the chops" and then "having restored my equilibrium" — by kicking somebody in the chops? Therefore the fellow is a murderous old fool, going about kicking people in the chops all the time? I have seen this happen to a translation. You should have heard it, the whole country came to a standstill for a week when those copies came over, and people were phoning each other: "Have you read page 712 where it says, "Rumi said to a bunch of cutthroats who were trying to stop a caravan, 'Cease your ...' " — I remember it because it was so climax-making — " 'Cease physically manifesting your anti-social behaviours in this manner which is inclement to the general conduct of affairs' " or something like that. Actually, he said to them, "Gumsho!" or "Get lost, fast!"

Except for a very nice fellow called Sayed el-Nafisi, who was professor of Persian at Tehran. There's a very famous story about him. He spent his life investigating the roots of the Persian language, and he discovered early fragments were in the Kuwisian and everything like that, on pots, and he spent twenty years studying — he was a very learned fellow, very nice fellow. Faisal Khan, who was Minister of Education at the time, invited him to Kabul. He arrived, and he got down from the plane — we didn't have walkways and all that sort of thing in those days, you just took your bags and walked in the general direction of town unless you had people meeting you. Anyway he was met by a wizened porter with an enormous rope — no trolleys in those days — you know the system — they just put all the rope through all the handles and they carried the whole lot. This fellow said to him, "May I carry your bags to where we can get a carriage for you?" The man almost had a heart attack, because this was the spoken archaic Persian which he had found on pots in the Black Mountains.

He took this fellow by the hand and brought him to the hotel, intent on sitting him down there and taping and recording everything he'd said. And to his amazement he discovered that everybody in the hotel and everywhere else was speaking the same. And it was like, to him, going back to the Elizabethan period in English.

He was a very nice fellow, I saw him about a week later and he was still reeling under the impact of writing down everything that everybody said, and I said, "Don't worry, because they all speak it, they're not going to go away."

That is the lighter aspect of translation or lack of it or something like that, but where the significant damage is done is where you get either phrases or terminology, or worse still, interpretations, which are not of an authentic nature. We can claim to have the original texts and authentic copies because it is so essential for the authentic works to be kept, and the authentic spirit, idea and intention behind them to be kept clear. Certainly, all over the East – and West for that matter – people have written interpretations and commentaries on commentaries and that sort of thing, but as long as there exists a corpus of basic books, reference can always be made back to them, or, at any given time, there are always a number of people around who know the texts so well that these can't be faulted.

Because apart from the actual knowledge that they carry, apart from the actual words strung together, the texts also carry the force of the energy with them. As with most objects made in the Tradition, they are imbued with the energy, the identification with the person, the love, or the rapport with the material they are using, and they put it into that thing. Now a good average artisan will do that automatically. If he's a good carpenter or painter or sculptor or weaver or potter or something like that, he likes his medium, he identifies with it, we would say he puts "some of himself" into it, yes. But in the Tradition, the thing is that there is something more put in, which is the energy.

So by the very writing, the stringing-together, the combination, the identification, put into writing these manuscripts; they are highly charged – and by miscopying or mistranslating or ignoring chunks of them – because they don't fit in with someone's particular idea or scheme or something like that – one is taking away a lot of the energy and the strength which is in there. Or you get the situation which applied for instance for a great many years in Victorian England, in which a lot of things were edited out—you know, covers were put around piano legs and things like that because of the "unmentionables"—when excising the sort of "robust" words or "robust phrases" was taken to a ridiculous degree—you get somebody who is translating, and who maybe doesn't like to use an anatomical term, so he cuts the whole thing down. If there is no text with which to compare that—then you have problems. Equally, if there is no formulation of music, sound, activity, exercise or other things in the Tradition with which to compare, then the thing can go completely askew.

It doesn't really do anybody any damage, but what it does do is take them off down the side streets and by-ways, and they get lost and confused and buffeted from pillar to post—but if they hang on to a main line of thought, if they understand the basic intention and impulsion of all the teachers, compare it with their own, and try and tag along with it, then inexorably they get pulled along the right direction. They are pulled in the sense that they're drawn or attracted—like attracts like. It doesn't mean to say that they're pulled in the sense that there's no effort from them. It is very often an effort to be pulled, because, at any given moment, a person can be pulled in different directions, by different things, for different purposes.

But if their priorities are right, and if they have something significant on which to rely, which is an abiding and long-lasting and sort of eternal basis of truth—measure things against that. Don't measure it against transitory things. Transitory things have a place: clothes, fashion, things like that, change. "Our forefathers wore things like that, therefore we should also." Well, this is so-called orthodoxy which can go completely askew: "We should not have electricity, telephones, cars, etc."—no. After all, I say myself, because I don't like anything to do with the sea or swimming or boats, or anything like that—"If I was intended to cross the sea, I would have had fins." But the answer to this, when some of the orthodox say, and I've heard it said, "If God had intended there to be things like electricity, He would have created people with luminous noses" or something, so that they could read without the necessity of light.

The answer to all that is that, after all, if one accepts the fact that God gave to man the ability to invent light, surely this can be taken to be at least a tacit acceptance of it. After all, if intelligence comes from God and man then develops that and benefits from it, this is a perfectly normal state of affairs.

It is when a person, for whatever reason, loses sight of the value of themselves, and treads a very narrow division between valuing themselves and over-valuing themselves — because there is a commonly-held thing, that one should be humble, meek and that sort of thing. Yes, nobody should be arrogant all the time, I mean I can be meek as all get-out if the situation demands it, but I can be arrogant as hell depending on the circumstance. If I use my arrogance in the wrong place, the least I get probably is a punch in the eye. If I go up to a drunk and say, "Get out of my way you horrid fellow, do you know who I am?" and he doesn't care really, and I can find out very quickly. So therefore, I, as I say, can be as meek as necessary — it doesn't mean to say that I become totally meek or totally arrogant at any given moment. There is a sort of curious ambivalent attitude: the "me, me, me, I, I," should be kept down or rather it should be kept balanced. It should be kept in proportion.

There is nothing wrong, in fact there is everything for, thinking about oneself, worrying about oneself, looking after oneself, developing oneself — not to the detriment of anybody else, or society in general. Not to the degree that a person becomes a predator, a menace, or something like that — no, because then they have to be put down. But a person has a responsibility towards themselves to develop themselves within a harmonious context. The teaching is there, the books are there, the continuity is there: this is the strongest guarantee — looking at the continuity of the teachers involved. This is the continuity of the quality, efficiency and usefulness of a teaching.

If you look at, say, the average political party — whether right, left or centre — every few years, or every one or two generations, there is an outstanding figure. "I remember the days of Lloyd George or Gladstone or x, y, or z" — all that sort of thing. These people may be very outstanding personalities, but people quote them because they're the exception rather than the rule. "In the country of the blind, the one-eyed man is king" — right. They say, "Good old Lloyd George" — I wouldn't give you a banana for Lloyd George, but by comparison, he was a giant among pygmies. At the present moment, for instance, you look at world leaders — which ones have the stature of what used to be called — a word which is never used now because it's too evocative: "statesmen"? Politicians, yes. Political leader, yes. A statesman is a completely different thing. A statesman is an international figure with international authority because of his knowledge, personality, wisdom, tact, and everything like that, not just because he happened to have conned his way by some sort of election to become President of something.

I say with all arrogance, that in our teaching we aim to maintain a standard of excellence — not just occasionally having a more erudite person surfacing, because otherwise how can we demand any higher standard from anybody else? If we have our troughs and valleys and slobbering about, and then throw up one fellow who is marvelous for fifty years or something like that, and then relax again down into a slumber — people will say, "Okay, we can do that, that's no big deal." On the law of averages, one's bound to throw up somebody occasionally who's got a little bit more *nous* than the average person. But just because the average people are a lot of slobbering idiots, and one person has one ear above the morass, it doesn't make him marvelous.

So if you have sustained excellence, you can pull up not only by your own efforts, but by relying very heavily on the energy and the teaching which is left behind for us to use. It was left for us to use, it wasn't to be left and put on a concrete plinth, and as you pass by you take your hats off and cross yourself — no, it's to be used, or it will mummify. And its energy will not be dissipated, but it will remain there, and it is a cosmically functioning, harmonious activity. As they say, nobody is forced to drink from the fountain. But if they don't, it is to their own detriment.

It's not a threat: "Drink, or else!" Either the impulsion is there, the need is there, the feeling is there, or it isn't. Yes, it can be engendered. I mean there are ways of sparking it off in a person, certainly, but it is better if a person somehow finds it, latches onto it, nourishes themselves from it.

And the continuity of doing that is there, it's not a great secret: we have the line of teachers, we have the line of descent, we have the genealogy, we have all the paraphernalia of it, it's demonstrable — you can go back three generations, see the books, the commentaries, the projection of the Teaching, and you'll find a constant. The only variation is within the people to whom it is taught. They have their ups and downs, but hopefully their ups and downs should even out. Okay, there is a certain vacillation, but if that evens out, you get a harmonious situation—harmonious within oneself, not a famous quote which I once heard from somebody—he wasn't a very illuminated person—he said, "These here philosophers are an awful dull lot."

Well, one doesn't have to be—it doesn't mean that by working on oneself or working internally one is going to eschew anything and feel shy and only giggle, or do nothing extraordinarily extroverted—that one should be sombre and generally dreadful. Because who wants to be really dreadful? I epitomize what I am supposed to be saying—if I go around painted dark brown, have a long beard, it could attract a certain amount of interest and comment—and a large number of loonies. I neither have the time nor the inclination to do that, apart from the fact that it's uncomfortable and cold and everything—but one can be in the world and not of the world without compromise to either thing: balanced, harmonious activity. That is all, really, one asks. But hold onto the link, hold onto the chain. That's what it's there for; that is what its purpose is.

Yes, we do of course, and can, and have, updated certain tactics, certain techniques, certain things. Sometimes one takes certain short-cuts. After all, time can be stretched or time can be telescoped, if you know how to do it. It can be telescoped in the sense that you can say, okay, I'll make a journey from A to B. Practically, in practical terms, by car or by plane, it'll take x number of days or x number of weeks—fine. Now is the purpose of this particular going from A to B what will happen between A to B or is it what will happen to the person at this point? If the purpose is to have various experiences between this—fine. If it is getting to B, one should and does use the quickest possible means to do it.

Equally, in terms of learning or transmitting energy—you can either say: "All right, a person can do this or that and build up a certain degree of energy. Or, if they're going to need that or if it would be beneficial for them to get it now, one can use such-and-such a technique to transmit it now by a particular activity. In that way, as I say, we can cut corners, not to get speed but to cut out the unnecessary. Because after all, by using the texts which we have, we are saving time and cutting corners. We're not expecting people to sit down and experience everything that all the great masters taught us; otherwise if they hadn't left it behind for us to use, they wouldn't have written it down. It is saving us time because they're giving us stuff in the form which we can readily assimilate and use.

As I've said before if you want to drive from A to B you don't sit down and invent and build a car; you take advantage of something which has already been done. There's no shame in doing that at all — "Oh, I should do it myself!" Yes, certain things, in terms of updating of techniques — yes. They do exist because they have to keep pace with the changing social and other situations, and if they are of value, you do them, there is just no question: "Is it which one, or what?" because the time has gone. It has to be "That person needs that, now or predictably in x." Therefore what are the possibilities? That one, so you do it.

Some people call it magic — it isn't, it's very technical. And it's useful. We have a technical teaching and we should use it.

Chapter 12

CONDITIONING

Immediate and unthinking reactions: Media-imposed reactions; Forms of indoctrination; Legitimate and harmful conditioning; How conditioning presupposes intellectual, economic, individual or social force-feeding; Freedom as a prerequisite; Difference between freedom and license, liberty and responsibility; Continuously updating one's understanding of harmonious development; How real development involves multiple focusing.

People are conditioned to react. Sometimes they don't stop to think: "Should I make that telephone call, do I have to, to whom?" What they're doing then is either reacting to the printed word – "It was in the papers, it must be true" or "I saw it on the telly" or "My favourite commentator" or something like that "said it, so therefore I must do it."

People are conditioned from the time they are children; they are, to a lesser and greater extent, indoctrinated, from the point of view of nationalism or religion or politics or other things. As I have said, a certain amount of conditioned thinking attitude is perfectly reasonable; a person should and does and must grow up and be told or understand either what nationality they are, or believe in, or what social status or family history there is – they must have certain terms of reference, points of view. But beyond a certain point, they have to learn, and they should be helped and taught to develop terms of reference of their own, and take up certain valid points of view on their own, have certain values of their own.

When I say they have to be taught, I don't mean that they have to be conditioned in the sense that they have to learn it by rote – that is it has to be told to them again and again and again, in that way of teaching. *The teaching means making information of all types available to them so that they can read through it, understand it, associate themselves with it, and find it valid.*

This doesn't come all at once – it doesn't come at any particular age, it doesn't depend on someone's degree of intellect or learning. It's a constant thing, developing all the time: points of view, terms of reference, and certain things based on certain significant values. They can be helped to develop these points of view and attitudes and understanding by explanation – not necessarily by interpolation or interpretation. A certain amount of interpretation always goes into explanations. Any explanation that you might hear from somebody about something – anything at all – has a certain amount of subjective quality in it. Supposing you ask ten people their opinions of a particular carpet – you will probably get ten different points of view, one of them might say, "We saw that carpet and the colour was horrible." That may be a subjective evaluation because they don't like that particular colour. If you're going to take that one interpretation and then say that that particular carpet is horrible, as are all other carpets like that, which may be Herati or Tabriz or something, as they have colours in common.

You haven't just been conditioned by that one phrase, because conditioning actually takes a much longer time, but in that little area of, if you like, appreciation of Herati or whatever carpets, they are terrible – because "somebody I know" or "whose opinion I trust" or "whose discernment I rely on" said, when asked what that particular carpet was like: "It's horrible." So that becomes a term of reference.

It doesn't mean to say that then you automatically have to examine, experience, analyse and doubt any explanation or anybody's opinion about anything. One can have and one does have and one should be encouraged to have, a certain amount of debate about certain things. After all, questions of art or taste can be very personal. I mean I personally don't at all like some Impressionist paintings – all right. I can fault them from my personal point of view: I don't like the arrangement, I don't like the colours used, I don't like the figures, I just don't like them – it's a personal thing. But if a particular artist has drawn something impressionistic, and if that artist is a true artist, a true draughtsman, then he has a right, having learnt all the necessary basics of painting or drawing or whatever, to then branch out to his own thing.

I take issue, for instance, and I did with great pleasure, in Paris many years ago when people were riding bicycles backwards and forwards across canvases in different colours and rolling on canvases covered in paint. That type of — I suppose, reluctantly, one could call it art, somehow, but I don't think a person doing that can really call himself an artist, he can be a painted gymnast rolling on the canvas covered in paint. I don't like Picasso for instance, but he was certainly without doubt a very excellent draughtsman and artist. What he wanted to draw after he had developed his techniques and cubism is his own right and privilege.

I'm not getting away from the subject. What I'm saying is: if I hate Picasso, that is a personal like or dislike of mine. This is an area where one can debate and people do debate ad infinitum about this kind of thing, and that's all right. I mean to say don't take any notice of him, he is a chocolate-box-pussycat man. Yes, I like pussycats on top of chocolate boxes and things like that — simple. But to debate about the scansion of a piece of poetry or something like this is perfectly viable, perfectly reasonable.

If you take up entrenched positions based on certain fundamental values, you don't compromise on those principles, that's all right — but you can have flexibility. There's a difference between flexibility and wandering about — what I call a sort of butterfly attitude, wandering from flower to flower. One of my great enemies in the world in general is conditioning; because it presupposes, in my experience, force which has been brought to bear upon an individual, upon a group or a society or a country — either political force, intellectual force, economic force or whatever force — which has more often than not pressured them into having a common attitude, a common reaction to certain things. There are areas where the human being, in order to properly express himself, properly fashion himself as far as he can, and properly develop himself in a harmonious way — must have freedom to do so.

Freedom is not license. The line between the two has become progressively blurred. "I can say anything I like because I'm a free man, this is democracy, and this is liberty" — no. You cannot say anything you like if it disturbs, frightens, or abuses anybody else. It is not just discourteous. It is license: it is infringement of another person's liberty. You can say right, we have the liberal arts, including poetry or playwrighting, and you can write a play which I suppose by average definition could be obscene, pornographic — this is not the correct exercise of liberty. This is not an old fogy, orthodox, point of view. Any infringement on the liberty of others is an abuse of your own so-called liberty.

When I talk about liberty of harmonious development — this liberty is also limited. It's limited by your responsibility, or a people's responsibility, or a country's or a universal responsibility. What do they want to obtain? What is their definition of liberty? What are the terms of reference that they use? And what are the truths by which they stand? If those are defined as far as the individual is concerned or as far as the community is concerned — if they are defined constantly and regularly, they do not take on the accretions or barnacles or rust and everything which obscure their true nature.

This is an aspect of the "green" truth or the "blue" truth — right. The colour of it is almost irrelevant. The basis of it is, say, one truth in different circumstances. It may appear in a different guise, colour, sense, meaning, or a different quality — but the basis is immutable. So what has that got to do with conditioning?

Well, you can get a person, a bunch of people, a community, or a country, and you can constantly hammer them with an aspect or an interpretation of something, to the point this is accepted as holy writ, chapter and verse, and that is "it" — right. You might argue and it has been argued, that one can take an aspect of, shall we say, harmonious development within a cosmic sense, and harping away on that constantly, you get that really fixed in people's minds. If it is based on a valid truth, then where is the harm? There is no great harm: but it is imposing a limitation, because you are giving a person or a people or a community what is called a blinkered vision — they are looking at that single thing.

Now, by definition, an intense and constant study of a truthful and harmonious concept cannot necessarily be bad — no. Unfortunately what happens is this: you then, if we are considering the one aspect, you must take into consideration one of the most confusing things which exists in the cosmos, and that is called the human intellect. What happens is this. There is a small portion of a truthful harmonious concept — right. Once that has been, shall we say, mastered, if the people have been conditioned into looking at that, they will use this great, profound and very so-called valuable intellect to penetrate, as they think, deeper and deeper and deeper into that particular concept, where in actual fact mastery of it to a much lesser degree is sufficient.

The next step is spreading out and penetrating the whole concept of a reasonably broad front – not an exaggerated front, because after all, concepts are linked, and they go in various directions, and it's very complicated. The human mind is like this – if you encourage people to specialize, it's quite good up to a point, but then the human beings will take over and they will over-specialize, and then they're specialized to the point that their participation is so refined, that they have literally no opportunity to exercise that.

I'll give you a very banal example, but such things happen, and it shows you. I had a cat which had an infection in its eyes, and I took it to the local vet and he didn't know what to do, so he gave me drops of this, that and the other thing, and I was away for a month, and when I came back the cat's eyes were in a very bad state, so I phoned around and I said who is the best cat man – and they said so-and-so. I took the cat to Reading and showed it to this fellow, and he said, "Ah, you want Professor so-and-so" and I said, "Fine, where is he?" and they gave me his telephone number. I phoned and said, "Can I speak to Mr. So-and-so?" – "What is it about?" And I said, "It's my cat." And so the man said, "I am Professor so-and-so, and I only deal with cats' eyes." And I said, "It's exactly what I want – cat's eyes." "Yes," he said, "but what is the matter with the cat's eyes?" "Well," I said, "It's inverted lids." He said, "I'll be there in five minutes." So he arrived, it wasn't five, it took him about twenty minutes. He arrived slavering, saying, "I have got a book about the inversion of cats' eyes." It was the actual truth – he was the greatest living expert on inverted eyelids, which make the eyelids turn in because the muscles are stretched, and when a cat blinks they flip up – what you have to do is operate on the muscles and just tighten them – and he was the greatest expert in the world and he had a book to prove it and he operated on the cat and it was perfectly all right.

Now, that, you might say, is marvelous, it was a great help and useful for that particular cat. But when he was there, he said, "You know, it's a good thing your cat didn't break a leg or anything, I wouldn't know what to do." Now that fellow was a veterinary surgeon, a professor of veterinary medicine, and he says, "I couldn't save the cat's leg" – but inverted eyelids, "Oh, marvelous." Now that is, as I say, an example; but it is a typical example, if you take it, about the intellectual area — this is the pattern of thinking: we must have experts and specialists in certain areas — certainly. But there's a point beyond which the specialization becomes so narrow that firstly, the areas themselves are very often forgotten. All the training which they use to get there — and then they don't have the ability to exercise that technique, or even to teach it.

So they have almost burnt out at that apex. That man is probably sitting by his phone waiting for inverted eyelids, whereas he could be down the road setting cats' legs, or whatever. As I say, it's a banal example, yet it is an example of over-specialization where a person will reach the pinnacle of his career and — all right, as far as that cat was concerned, it was marvelous that there should be such a person — but he could have spread himself a bit more widely, and been able to teach.

So, all this rambling really means is this, that unfortunately if you encourage the human intellect, educational system, cultural climate, to over-investigate certain areas based on certain terms of reference which they have taken and refined further and further, it is not actually developmental in the way that we consider it in the Tradition. *Developmental means not just a narrowing focus, but a focus on different levels simultaneously, going between one and the other, or harnessing two or three, in the same way that when one uses a hand, one is harnessing several muscles, sinews and things at the same time.* Certainly, one can develop one muscle in a specifically difficult way and allow the others to atrophy. That is of little use — I mean, I've got the most developed trigger finger in the world — well, that's great, but how do you peel an apple? Which is better, to peel an apple or develop a trigger finger? — well this is a debate which people debate about all the time.

Uncritical acceptance of so-called experts in certain fields is perfectly all right. People will quote me again: "Ah, you always say, for instance, you don't have to rediscover this or that, or know how it works for it to do you good." No, but that's fine in an area where a degree of development has been achieved, and the spin-off in all the antibiotics and so on, continue. You can and do uncritically accept certain things, but in certain areas, questions have to be asked and answers have to be sought. Questioning or asking does not necessarily mean doubting or challenging: "I don't believe that" or "How can I believe that" or "Should I believe it?"

In the Tradition, terms of reference are available. The widest spectrum of them exist under all sorts of circumstances, and nobody has ever said or written that one should abandon or try and fight some of the basic, valuable and necessary conditionings that people get through normal education, upbringing, and social, economic and any other contact — they're all perfectly necessary.

But one does have the right — and not only the right, but the responsibility to oneself — to be on a quest, on a journey of understanding and discovery of harmonious development as a result of getting answers to one's questions. Not answers that feed in the question and out comes the answer, and then one assimilates the answer and goes on to question number 2 or 3. Some of the questions are best unasked, some of the answers are better just listened to and not thought about. And then you say, "Well, that comes precious near conditioning" — no, because conditioning as I say is imposition of certain terms of reference, willy-nilly, whether one feels it or not. Whether one gets any feedback from the answer or not, one accepts them. "The British are like this" — I myself, in one part of me, I am a creature of conditioning when I am an Af: "We Afghans are like that, and that's it" — finish.

And they don't brook any contradiction on that basis — we will accept that somebody else who says, "We Egyptians are like that" — because if we're on that level of Neanderthal nationalism, fine, then there's no argument. "We're like that, we're like this" — fine, what do you do? Walk away, shake hands, fight, or do nothing. So this isn't terribly critical. It's when that attitude indicates a course of action which indicates an action which is inharmonious, that you're using the wrong term of reference or point of view.

If you go to a dinner party and put your elbow in your neighbour's soup, and he said, "I say, that's not on," and you say, "We Afghans always do that" — you don't get invited again. This is the wrong thing to do at the wrong time — the wrong card to play, it's impolite, and it does little to enhance the reputation of Afghans in general. So you don't do it. Unless you're very clumsy, it's no great problem to avoid putting your elbow into other people's soup. You don't say, "I am a free man, this is a share-owning Democracy, I'll put my thumb in your ear if I feel like it" — no. Because that is then trespassing on somebody else's liberty —

to prevent yourself from aggressing somebody else is not diminishing
your own liberty, this is an unjustified thing.

If the press or the television or the political parties or any party of
any group, impose their opinion on other people because they're understandably blowing their own trumpet—that is not to say that one
goes around with a sort of haunted look, looking over one's shoulder,
expecting to be conditioned, trying to avoid it at all costs and that sort
of thing—people are worried enough already. They're not exchanging
one conditioning for another, because they say, "Ah yes, you become
one of these Sufis, all they do is replace the conditioning." No, the conditioning the average person has, has been taken on or imposed on them
without them exercising very much critical faculty—because either it
wasn't necessary or it was inconvenient or there was no alternative.

The terms of reference or writing or points of view or other things
in the Tradition are things which are explained to people for them to
accept, with the amount of critical ability which they can bring to bear.
They have to basically feel something for what they're taking on, and
believe it will be developmental for them. There's no outward sign or
promise or anything like that in nature—it doesn't exist and won't exist.
It is a person's responsibility to sort out the wheat from the chaff, and
not antagonize themselves when in the process of doing so. In case that's
a very mystical or complicated thing, this is a phrase which you hear, or
which you say: "I'm fighting with myself"—"Which of me is dealing
with my negative aura?"—all that sort of thing.

People antagonize themselves very often because, supposing
there's a significant degree of conditioning in one particular area, and
the person is conscious of this. You're not particularly happy with it,
it's not too terrible—they take another thing, say, from the Tradition,
and they impose that on the basic conditioning. That will inevitably
provoke a certain amount of hostility. You can't say, well this thing from
the Tradition is heavier than that bit of conditioning, therefore it's better—or alternatively, it's lighter, therefore it's more airy, therefore it's
more valuable—and that sort of imposition.

If you don't condition yourself, you don't persuade yourself out of
one into another in the sense that you've swapped one conditioning for
another using a critical judgment which you're building up, so that imperceptibly, it doesn't creep up on you: you suddenly wake up in the

morning and you're thinking in a completely different way—no. *Your innate common sense has compared it, found it harmonious, and allowed it in.* You might say, "Years ago, I didn't consider that a tasbee was anything more than a string of beads." Well if there was a point where somebody said: "You will not consider this to be a string of beads, you will consider this to be a fantastic item of use, and there is a terrible conflict within you and then you accept it to be so although all your conditioning's against it"—forget it.

Don't precipitate situations like that. Take it, it may be a string of beads. And they may be very nice and they may mean something and people use them, and one develops a harmony with them and one uses them and it becomes a harmonious part of your nature. If you impose it on yourself, you're risking the so-called tussle with yourself, battle with yourself. You've got to understand that twenty or thirty or forty or fifty years of conditioning is not wiped away in so many months, and not all of it has to be wiped away. It's just that some things have to be phased out, other things have to be phased in—but things which harmonize with you.

What I say is usually reasonable common sense, but you don't have to think only in—I was going to say in my terms, but that's a bit difficult—you don't have to say for instance: "What would my teacher do under those circumstances?" Because you'd commit an error—you would never know, and it might be something very ridiculous or extraordinary, and therefore you don't—that is a conditioning from the subjective point of view, and it doesn't work. You don't condition yourself, you harmonize with yourself. You accept terms of reference, points of view, things, people, places, with which you feel a rapport—you don't necessarily have to explain why.

You certainly don't have to explain to yourself why in conventional terms of reference: "I went to such-and-such a place and I felt, kind of, well, like, wild" or this or that. Well, you knew you felt something, you thought something, you had some feeling.

Don't fall into the trap of trying to recondition yourself. Assimilation by harmony is one thing. Imposition is another. Imposition is the easiest thing, and it provokes the most problems, especially if it is a hostile, limiting, or imprisoning inquisition. Because people are always trying to break out of it—they don't necessarily know how or what particular thing is menacing them. They just know that something is wrong. The moment they can feel a harmony with something which they feel has the basis of a developmental path or phase in it, they will latch onto it and slot in with it.

So you don't put up a great barrier against everything and everybody in case they might be deepening the conditioning. You maintain an average, reasonable attitude towards various things — you exercise your critical faculty where it's necessary, and in areas where you have some terms of reference or expertise.

The rest you don't worry about.

Chapter 13

UNDERSTANDING SPIRITUALITY IN THE TRADITION

The Spiritual aspect in the Tradition; The parallel nature of activities; Transmission of refined energy.

The basic reason for the existence of the Tradition or its functional purpose, is to spread knowledge among people, and for them to learn this knowledge and/or body of techniques and use them in a physical, practical way — so that they think about them, read about them, talk about them, use them, and let this teaching or philosophy become a part of them, as they become a part of the philosophy by their adhesion to or membership of a group.

You have the practical area, in which people congregate, and they talk and exercise and discuss things. There are other areas of activity, where we produce things like a newsletter, and encourage people to write in it in order to make contact with other groups. We also encourage people to travel in order to make contact with other groups, and to find, not only like-thinking people in the sense that they also think with the terms and the points of view which we use in the Tradition, but people of perhaps similar backgrounds, similar lifestyles, similar ages, similar problems, children, etc. — so that they can identify more readily with other groups.

It is perfectly all right and quite normal for one to say, "Well, we have various groups in Argentina, Brazil, Germany, France, and so forth" — by corresponding, meeting or travelling with those groups or individuals, those groups become actual entities, they become people: they are called by their various names and one knows them as that person. One remembers the conversation or the meeting one had with them, and this develops a stronger and deeper relationship between the groups — on a practical level to begin with, and then on a deeper level — because if two or more people are thinking about or working towards the same goal, or trying to understand the same things — both in a practical sense: discussing it, "What do you think about it?" or "What is your attitude towards it?" — in a deeper sense, two or three or five or ten people pool their energy in a way which is impalpable: it doesn't have to be obviously present. *The very fact that they're on the same wavelength creates a pool of energy and helps them to transmit energy, force and ideas to each other, and distribute them among different groups.* This is a very practical, solid, useful, and necessary function.

Another function which is equally as practical — but from the point of view of semantics, sometimes people divide it, or put it into a different realm — is the spiritual aspect of the Tradition. There is no difference in the sense that the spiritual and the practical, the social and the spiritual, prayer, a *zikr* — *are all participative activities, they all require energy and effort, and they produce an effect.*

In the specifically spiritual aspect of the Tradition, a person does not start out, or sit down at a given moment, and say: "Right, I am now going to be spiritual for the next half-hour" or something. Define your terms of reference. As I said before, I'm always talking about the necessity of getting rid of a certain amount of conditioning which has been imposed on people. People are taught to think in this way or that way because they are "men" or "women," or because they come from a particular social or economic background, or a particular country, or family influence or whatever — right.

I was mentioning that one aspect of conditioning which exists in the East and doesn't exist in the West is the concept of a teacher or a Master. As I said then, in many countries or in Occidental countries, the idea of "Master" equates with "master and slave," superior/inferior, and then spins off into any conditioning which a person might think of — whereas in the Orient if one uses the term "Master," this is accepted without reservation, without there being the Western concept of inferior/superior: the know-all and the learner.

We all learn: everybody learns, there is no end to learning. So when one talks about the spiritual context, not the spiritual aspect — because if you say "aspect," then the semanticist will say to you, "Ah, you mean there is the practical aspect, which is driving from A to B and meeting people and saying 'How are you,' and eating together — and then there is the spiritual aspect — how do you eat spaghetti spiritually?" And of course people will delight in debating this, which is really fruitless, be-

cause the motivation of these people who have met together for the purpose of eating spaghetti, talking, and so forth and so on, implies
automatically a degree of preparedness either to engage in a spiritual
discussion, or to have a spiritual relationship, communion, or so forth.
The things are not divided – "We will not be spiritual."

So when I say a person does not or should not necessarily sit down
and say: "Now I am going to be 'spiritual', therefore I am going out of
life or out of a particular context – one is, in the Tradition, going
through and involving oneself in all the contexts which exist. *We are in
the world and not of the world.* There's no "switch-on" and increase the
spirituality: you know, "Just give a good jolt – Wow! – I mean that was
real spiritual!" This can be enhanced, this can be produced, this can be
imagined, this can be stimulated, one can exist on a permanent spiritual
high – or one can, in a harmonized way, tune into a spiritual activity
which is completely part of the everyday activity which one is doing.

Again, I repeat this – it's a cliché, but it does happen: "How does
one spiritually catch a bus?" The answer is: you do not. If the bus happens to be being driven by the Archbishop of Canterbury, it is possible
that standing at the bus stop holding a crucifix might predispose him to
stop for you or wait for you or charge you little or less than usual. But
really there is no such thing as – I think in fact it was the Bishop of Bath
and Wells who said: "Let us get on the spiritual bandwagon." I'm sure
he is a very good and saintly man, fortunately, I have not yet met him,
so I can't measure the degree of his asceticism or lack of it – but the
point being, really, that one doesn't switch on and switch off.

There are different levels of activity, existence, behaviour, thought,
reaction – which are parallel. They complement each other. On occasions, the physical presence of a person in a particular place will, because of the nature of the place – or because of the physical presence
in a gathering, because of the nature of the gathering or the quality of
the gathering – will boost or push through, or make a very strong contact with a deeper sense within the person, which may be one of the
levels of spirituality.

To sit down and say: "I am going to be spiritual for the next fifteen
minutes: can be a degree of arrogance. It depends how it's said, in what
context, or where. A person might take me to task, and say: "Now look,
if you go to a place, or you're in a situation which is manifestly full of a

certain quality of energy, surely you have every right to sit down and say, "I am going to feel spiritual" – not necessarily, "I am going to have a spiritual experience" – but "This is a place of a certain quality with which I identify, and I am going to have it."

There is a sort of nuance here when I say there's a degree of arrogance, in that it is better for the person, having identified a place, a situation, or being together with a person, to say: "I aspire to, I would like to – have or feel a spiritual quality in this place or in this circumstance." The arrogance comes – maybe this is unfair or uncharitable – in the "I am going to" which means that "I have the capacity to." Like somebody who says, "I've got three minutes, now tell me all about everything" which means automatically, "I will be able to understand."

Most of the activities within the Tradition, whether they may be the more obvious ones – exercises, zikrs, prayers, recitations, readings, other things – have a spiritual parallel existence. The ones which are not obviously or overtly of a spiritual nature, still have that. How do you increase the spiritual context of a situation? Do you sort of boost yourself up and connect? No, because usually, again, in the Western connotation, you are boosting yourself up to experience something – right. Again, in a Western connotation, when you say, "I am going to" or "I want to have a spiritual experience," in the West, a spiritual experience is almost defined for you already.

You will see a statue of the Madonna move or waggle her ears at you or something, and that will be a "spiritual experience." – Or a person will get knocked out or something. There are certain things, which, unfortunately, have been put down as being "spiritual experience" – and other things which are considered not to be spiritual experiences because, they are intangible. There are even books, you look it up: "My left kneecap fell off" – right. "That is spiritual experience number sixteen." I exaggerate mildly, not totally – people are actually told what type of spiritual experience is better than others.

A person can have a spiritual experience by putting themselves in tune, harmonizing with a place, a circumstance, or what they're doing, and have this spiritual experience which can pass almost without conventional notice. You don't have a blank sheet, and every time you have spiritual experience it leaves a thumbprint, so that at the end of the year you look up and you say: "Wow! That must have been a great year, I don't remember much about it, but somehow it was great."

Spiritual experiences are, by definition, of a personal nature. A person's search for, explanation of, relationship with God – is a personal thing. It doesn't affect everybody in the same way. There is no measure by which you say, "Well, that was a spiritual experience B on the Richter scale – my teeth fell out" or "didn't fall out" so therefore it wasn't very great. People feel it, people record it, people often remember it afterwards – there are situations which are provoked in the Tradition where a person or a group of people might visit a place or have a spiritual experience of very great intensity, which, if it was felt to the intensity that it exists at that time, would probably knock them out. It wouldn't be dangerous, drive them mad, do them any harm or anything like that – but the intensity of it would be so much that it has to be spread out over a period and diluted, so that they then recall part of it subsequently, over the next few weeks, months, or years – and they think that was extraordinary, that was significant, that was something.

Don't again, explain it: "I should have understood it at the time" – "Why didn't I understand it?" – no, because again, this is going back to the old *mea culpa* syndrome: "I am stupid." No – it's inefficient. Suffice it to say that when being alert and open to experiences of a useful nature – a person records them, remembers them: nothing is forgotten. It may not seem useful or it may not surface at that moment – that doesn't mean to say that it has not been useful. After all, on a practical, very banal level, every week you put away two pounds – you save two pounds – for something: to buy something, to pay the gas bill, to pay the electricity bill – something like that. After you've put the two pounds in your savings account, you don't immediately expect something to happen.

You say, "Ah, but that's a different thing, because I know that two pounds and two pounds and two pounds will produce such-and-such at the end of the year. That is on a banal level. Why not accept, on a more sophisticated level, that the investment of energy, over a period of days, weeks, months, years, better fits a person for situations when they may need it – whether it be in terms of physical, spiritual or other energy? It is no less valid, that they don't feel it now.

This is one of the great diseases of the Western – I hesitate to use the word "civilization" but I suppose one should – "We want it now." People have said to me: "I visited such-and-such a place, it was very nice, and it didn't do anything ... I'm still sort of me." Well, what did you expect to be? The Archangel Gabriel? We already have one. No, I'm sorry, this isn't the way the thing works. There isn't an examination at the end of each term.

People feel and know, or should know, that they are investing their time, energy, attention, dedication, and their discipline in something which means, and must mean, something to them – otherwise, if they don't believe that, or if they don't accept that, or if they can't accept that, then they should be in some other activity where they can. If they're looking for tangible signs, for instance, the itching of the shoulder-blades which shows the emergence of wings – if they're waiting for that, they will wait a long time. There are angels who don't have wings. There are angels who have harps and are singularly discordant in their musical abilities, but they are not measured as musicians. It's a very nice idea: angels sitting on clouds, Cherubim and Seraphim and all that sort of thing are a necessary and useful and attractive and decent and desirable part of civilization – and why not? But if everything has to be judged by that, then one is losing sight of the fact that there is a building-up of different things.

You build up a harmony with other people, in that it will enable you to work with other people. You build up an understanding of certain exercises, activities, technical terms, and other things, in order that you may be able to use them. You build up a familiarity with activities so that you can see how and when and where they fit in – at the right time, at the right place, in the right proportion. There isn't, there will never be, and there cannot be, a collection of plus doubles and/or minus doubles in the sense of the Tradition.

You take any book – Hafiz, Jami, Saadi, Salman-i-Farsi, Jalaludin, or records of their lives, and go through it, day by day, week by week, do what they did, say what they said and dress as they dressed – and you become a latter-day Jalaludin Rumi as far as what you're saying, where you're travelling, where you're living is concerned – but we already have a Jalaludin Rumi. We don't need another one in those terms.

He left examples of what people should do — there's a verse which
he writes against himself, "The day when honest shopkeepers will fall
to the ground in reverence of Rumi will be the day when they don't
know Rumi" — which for the simple-minded among you, means that he
wasn't building a Rumi cult. He was teaching people how to be, if you
like, an updated Rumi. You might say that Rumi's a difficult enough
act to follow without being an updated Rumi, but he didn't say so.

*Spirituality is not a frame of mind. It is a tactic, a harmonious tactic,
which is used in contexts, in places, at moments when a person feels that
spirituality present in him. The very intangibility of the spirituality is its
defense.* If one could buy spirituality — and, goodness knows, the Bor-
gias tried and they didn't make it — or buy pseudo or positional
spirituality, "He is the great Whodunnit, therefore he must be marvelous" — no. This is Hafiz — "The humility of the teacher is born of his
arrogance."

Again, in order to prevent the porridge-brains stirring this through,
what happens is that the more one knows, the more humble one gets,
because the more respect one has for the people who have, as we say,
"touched the sky" and realized how insignificant they are, without then
going into this great thing, "Oh, I am so humble it isn't true" — that in
itself is an arrogance.

Anyway, there were the three monks: Benedictine, Jesuit and Car-
thusian. And they were debating their various strengths and weaknesses
and so forth, and the Dominican said at the end, "Well, we must all
admit that those Jesuits, in terms of logic, argument, knowledge, are
the greatest. But as far as we Dominicans are concerned, as far as
humility is concerned, we are the best."

A person, as I say, feels a spirituality or a humility — part of it is
gratitude. Gratitude is an aspect of both humility and spirituality. When
one sees somebody who is more unfortunate than one is, one says,
"There but for the grace of God, go I." But it is not necessary only for
this thought to be provoked by seeing some unfortunate person and
being grateful for the fact that one isn't as unfortunate as that. I mean
the very fact that I can reach out and pick something up should and
does give me cause for gratitude. There are millions of people who,
either physically cannot do that, or who, even if they could do it, are
blind, and it wouldn't do them any good. Therefore in little things like

that — it doesn't mean to say one is constantly on one's knees, but it is part of the parallel existence of that gratitude, which is part of spirituality, in the sense that, how does one then increase that spirituality?

The nearness to God, the comprehension of God, the comprehension of Man's place in the Cosmos, whether he means anything at all in the Cosmos, whether there are different worlds, what are they, and all these other questions — are all very useful and interesting, and I'm not saying that one should not think about or discuss them.

In the Tradition, this is a philosophy of use and learning. It explains things. If one reads enough, learns about things, they fall into place. Something which one has read or learnt months or years ago, again, explains something to one, maybe months or weeks later. If one has read something, or learnt a couplet or a quotation, and one goes about saying, "I'm going to use it" — you've got the tension build-up, and the person is saying, "I can't use it, it's useless" or "I'm useless" or "It doesn't work" — but if it's there, which it is, at some time it comes together, with a harmony on another level.

Now, strangely enough — this was pointed out to me at great level — that's not a Freudian slip when I say at great level, because I was unfortunate enough to be sitting with a German physicist in a plane, and we were flying from somewhere, and I was there for four hours next to him. And I made a remark about parallels, and of course, he "controlled" my thinking in the sense that "parallels never meet." I was flying from Alaska to some Scandinavian place — I think it was Stockholm — anyway, it was a very long flight, and after I had said, out of light-headedness, the classic thing of saying that the parallels do communicate — he said, "By definition, the parallel ..." and he had rimless glasses, as well, and I thought, "Oh brother!" so I made an excuse, and I went back, and there was a very sympathetic air hostess, and I said, "Would you kindly give this gentleman a constant supply of straight vodka — the moment he's finished it or whatever, just give it to him." So after half an hour he was paralytic, and that was fine.

The thing is this: that by certain terms of reference, parallels do not meet. But in that they exist, in the same context, in the same area — there is a communication between them. They are not insulated from each other so impenetrably that they just go on and on until the end of the world, otherwise you'd just get sort of shells.

So you get an activity, an energy, acting on one level—a level of spiritual contact, a level of awareness of a person, a place, a situation. Now, you have three levels. Those levels, at one point, will come together—not converging, because parallels don't converge—but communicating, so that the spirituality and the person or the context and the place will communicate across—and you will get a jump across and an impact, a situation.

This is not a fault of circuit—it is that certain things must, for their own good, be kept separated, because one doesn't need the constant contact of all the levels operating all the time, otherwise, as I say, one would make a "spiritual" choice of bus, rather than seeing that it's the 82 bus, that's where I want to go. At that point life could become very meaningful and complicated. So, in defiance of logic or whatever, they reserve the right to stay parallel and relate when the situation demands. If three or four of them relate at the same time, you get what we call in a technical term, "*takkan*": it's "shake"—where actually a person can experience a shake.

There is a third energy—which is produced actually by the Tradition itself, and it is available to individuals and to groups—of different qualities. If you like to put it into sort of physical terms—when you flex a large muscle, you use a very low type of energy. In using, for instance, sight, thought, hearing and touch, there is a much more delicate type or a very purer form of energy which is used. And in the more profound areas, within the Tradition, *we aim at producing and using a very, very refined, very pure energy, which is jealously guarded because it's difficult to produce, and it really is only used drop by drop.*

Q: Referring to the parallels that you were talking about; is there energy from one parallel to another, higher to the lower?

A: No. What happens is that although by definition, parallels exist like this, there are channels between all these parallels. When a situation occurs, when communication this way is necessary, the energy jumps or sparks across from one to the other, and causes—not a short-circuit, but a communication between two or three or four, or however many are involved in that particular situation.

There are sources, for instance, of very highly refined energy—there are hot spots on the surface of the earth where this is stored and distributed. It's received or sent off by groups or by individuals, and it's a micro-millisecond transmission of a specific type of energy. There have been occasions when people have physically stepped between transmission and reception of this type of energy, and have been knocked out for a few minutes. Physically, it's usually put down to heat exhaustion or a faint or something like that. It doesn't do anybody any harm—but sometimes it happens. You just have to be quick on your feet.

So, anyway, as I say, one doesn't decide on a particular degree or situation of spirituality as long as a person or a group maintains an awareness, an openness. They are receptive to these aspects of spirituality, or the impact which this energy may create upon them at a given moment. There are situations and circumstances where the transmission of this energy can take on unconventional forms—I'm not speaking of the unfortunates who might come between a transmission and reception—but ways of transmission. We have artifacts in the Tradition which are used in this way—there are places which are used, there are things which are made and sent to stay for two years, five years, fifty years, a hundred years, a thousand years, and that sort of thing—after being charged up to give off energy at a given moment.

There are activities or actions which a teacher may do which may be unconventional in Western terms, but which are for purposes of creating a circumstance, modifying a circumstance, or transmitting energy.

Chapter 14

INTEGRATING THE TRADITION INTO THE CONTEMPORARY WORLD

Tradition as an axle; Impossibility of compressing experience; Mental preparation for experience; Danger of pre-judging experience; Harmonizing with and imitating the balance of nature; Position of the Tradition in today's world; Tactics as flexible verbal and other communication; Role of technology; Responsibility for energy distribution and responsibility for control of such energy; How keeping people in ignorance is used as a means to dominate them; Giving and being an example to people outside the Tradition; Relationship with external world; Influencing people in a positive way; Geodetic and climatological factors; How dominating a situation creates envy and jealousy; How energy seeks its user.

If a person looks at anything: a country situation, a city situation, or any situation at all, and in some way they have decided even before the experience exactly what they would learn from that experience: they can miss a lot of the depth of that experience. They may in fact impose on themselves a limit to that experience. But if they are in a state of receptivity there are areas of benefit which do open to them. If you decide that a certain experience will not be good for you, it will not be good for you. If you believe that a certain experience will benefit you, the useful effect of that experience will be significantly increased. There is nothing of a superstitious nature in this, it is a concrete technical fact. The impulse or the movement can come from you, and you establish a momentum, and once that momentum is established, it needs just a little constant impact to keep going.

Think of a wheel turning. The wheel is the whole activity; and energy and activity gives it a "touch" to keep it turning. But in order that a wheel may run true, it needs an axle. That axle for you can be the Tradition.

Everything, cosmologically, is related to movement — harmonious, balanced, equilibriated. Man can, and does, disturb the balance of nature. He can profit from nature, he can use nature, he should take nature as his ally. There is no collision of values. So put together, harmonize, with everything which is cosmologically balanced. There is nothing mysterious, curious, magical, about this tactic.

I would now like to talk about the position and the integration of the Tradition in the world today. The actual position and the intention of the Tradition does not change, but it must have flexibility because of the changing social, political and other considerations. To communicate in former times, we used verbal communication and other communications which were correct for the time. In primitive times we used primitive techniques, even though we had more sophisticated techniques which we could have used. Primitive techniques were used because they didn't appear to be anything strange or hostile. In the present day of course, we use the existing technological advances to maximum effect: television, video, satellite communication, and all the other things. These are used for the spread and diffusion of information about the Tradition.

But we must have a parallel system of communication, and that is the communication between people. *For communication between people, we use a very essential and sophisticated thing, which is energy. Energy can be transmitted and received by instruments;* it can be stored and used by instruments and machines in a cold and technical way, because they are machines. The energy which is transmitted and received among human beings is warmer in character. It can be received, transmitted and stored, and it is used according to the ability of the person to use it. Each individual or each group in an area stores energy, and at the correct time and in the correct manner, they use this energy.

As I have said before, they are not told how much energy they have at any particular time. *All they know is that they are in contact with the Tradition. The stronger their contact is with the Tradition, the more energy can pass between them and the Tradition, and the more usefully they can store and use the energy in the region.* They have the responsibility to increasingly develop their relationship with the Tradition, but they should not worry about whether they are distributing it in the right way at the right time, because it is my function to control that distribution. I can only function really correctly if they are functioning correctly.

Various areas of the world are in different stages of development and evolution. The two areas that probably influence people most are the political and the economic, because political and economic situations also influence the social situations. Unfortunately, present-day economic and political situations are producing enormous tension almost everywhere in the world; and tension is the great enemy. It blocks the balanced and harmonious transmission of energy and it prevents its harmonious use. This happens in individuals, you can see it. Individuals compose groups, and groups compose countries, so the tension increases. *It is the responsibility of people in contact with the Tradition to maintain their tranquility in tension situations.* You're not responsible for saving the whole population of the area in which you live. You are responsible for your family, your group, and those who are close and dear to you. So, in a very positive way, you have to protect them.

When I mention the need for unity and protection, I'm not prophesying some cataclysm, but I am saying that the signals coming from all parts of the world point to increasing tension. Social imbalance, economic problems, political fighting for position and pushing, produce constant changes in balance. Years ago, and not many years ago, the amount of positive or negative influence was judged by the size or wealth of a country. Nowadays almost any country, however small, can create tension or terror situations. The human balance which used to be maintained has been lost; different countries make political claims against other countries. They back up these claims by force of arms and no matter how small these countries are, they will be encouraged or backed by one country or another.

How does this situation influence the Tradition? It does not influence the Tradition, but it influences people in the Tradition. The degree of tension is so high on this planet at the moment, that any disaster, natural or industrial, creates a wave of fear throughout the world. Nobody really trusts their rulers or their heads of state. The average person doesn't understand the international political poker game, and if people don't understand something they get nervous about it.

An old trick of control is to keep people in ignorance: ignorance of the political situation or the economic situation of the country. And finally, when every other excuse has been used, very often the people who are responsible for the situation just vanish. So what do we do, how to we react to these changing circumstances? I will give you what seems to be a simple solution. *Maintain and develop your contact with the Tradition.*

Certainly, in whichever country you live, you can't ignore the situation around you. The temptation is very great to involve yourself socially, politically, and in an active fashion in other ways in order to improve the situation or bring about a change. This is perfectly understandable and reasonable, but take into consideration two facts: firstly, I can assure you, in the Tradition we have professionals. For at least eleven centuries professionals from the Tradition have been working in Europe; they have established methods and ways of pressuring. They keep — as they have to keep — a low profile. Sometimes their association with the Tradition becomes known, and, unfortunately as a result, their activities become limited. What you can do as individuals, in your family, among your friends and in your work, is to give an example and be an example.

That doesn't mean going around trying to argue, convince or convert people to your way of thinking. Because they say, "Yes, this is another socio-political or cult situation." And they will discuss and dispute and argue with you on a socio-political cultish level. That is not to say that you cannot talk about or admit to being in the Tradition to people outside. An example in a family or a group or a work situation, if your example is an obviously good one, attracts attention. If you are calm and balanced in a crisis, people will notice this consciously or subconsciously, and they will perhaps ask themselves how or why. They will either say to you, for instance, what tranquilizers are you taking? Or how do you keep calm in a crisis? Well, you either tell them the truth: such-and-such a tranquilizer or Jalaludin Rumi, depending.

A person who is receiving energy from the Tradition shows it not only by their actions, but on a very much deeper and more basic level, and that transmission is picked up by other people. Because while their interior being may not be developed in any way, it is sill functioning — although slowly — and it gradually provokes the person into looking at or watching somebody. So, consciously you can give an example and subconsciously transmit it. You can try it, practically. If there is a situation which is perhaps negative, or might become negative, or could become more positive — look or concentrate or direct your thoughts at a person in that group: a person whom you think either might be the source of any negative energy, or who might be able to help you to improve the positive nature of that ambience or meeting. You use a very simple technique: you direct your thoughts toward them. You think towards them.

You do not fix them with a stare and glare at them. If you are a man and you do that, and the person you are staring at or glaring at is a woman, you might get a punch in the eye from her husband or boyfriend and the negativity of the situation will increase. If it is a person in your family or your group or your work that you know; you know what they look like so you get a mental picture of them, and you send, by directed intention, a positive influence. This can be done very quickly or instantaneously by immediately visualizing for instance a positive thing or a positive place; or if you have more time, you repeat a *zikr* or a phrase — something positive. You can see it work depending on how precise your thought transmission is.

When you're doing that you don't let your own emotions interfere: "I won't look at that person or I won't visualize them because I don't like them." The same effect happens, only negative. You're thinking of that person and bringing out a negative and a negative is going out. For that fraction of a second or for that minute, you have to detach yourself, focus, transmit, and come back into the situation. You can use a number of artificial ways of getting that few seconds: you can cough or you can sneeze or you can drop something on the floor to break the conversation, or to give you those two or three seconds that you need. That is one way of influencing a person in a situation.

Equally, the presence of a person in a place or a situation can have a similar, more diffused, larger influence. It's a slightly different technique, but similar. If there are 100, 150, 200 or two thousand people, you don't have to visualize all two thousand of them, or look at each one of the two thousand individually, for obvious reasons. You visualize the situation. If it is a larger group or area or place — a similar technique. You can use this technique many times during the course of a meeting, or during the course of a day or a week of a month, and you should try and feel the result coming back. It's not always possible to feel it, it may come back in a way which is not the way you actually expect. The thing you do not do is to wait for it to come back. You do not do it and then look at the person to see if anything is happening. If you use it on successive occasions you develop the ability to do it.

There are some people and some situations which are very difficult indeed to make a connection with. The connection depends on a very large number of factors. It can depend on climatic, geological, geodetic, any number of factors. Literally, a person can be sitting five metres away and because of a geological change in the earth, the transmission is diverted so, therefore, that is just one of the reasons why you don't wait or look for the feedback, because if you're sitting there trying to influence a person or a situation and the transmission isn't getting through, and you're waiting for the feedback — you get more and more tense, and eventually you go over and shout in that person's ear.

You have to be sensitive to the situation, understand it, see how you relate to it, because you are also a part of it. This is one of the ways, in the present situation, we can help to influence things gently. I advise you: leave the big battles to the professionals. By not doing that, one can attract hostile attention, and by attracting a certain amount of antagonism, the positive which you are giving out or trying to give out, can be cancelled out by the negative coming from other people. We do not need martyrs: political, social, economic or any other. We have professional martyrs. We have the most professional martyrs there are, and they're called Malamatis*.

If you, individually and as groups, can manufacture, receive and store energy — manufacturing it by the *zikrs* and exercises which you have been given — receiving the energy by contact with the Tradition; increasing the amount you receive and can use by developing: you can affect those people and things around you more efficiently and significantly. It is not a magical or superstitious activity, it is a technical training, but it does not work unless you are harmonized with the situation you are trying to influence. It does not work if you do the right thing at the wrong time. The techniques which you use must be flexible so that they can be applied according to the situation. You should only be influenced by the situation in your choice of technique; you should not be motivated by the situation.

*A Sufi order

You should create an influence in a situation or in a place without dominating the situation, because firstly, the moment you dominate a situation you create envy and jealousy. Secondly, this domination can in some ways be exciting to you, and some people can go on an adrenaline trip. The secret is the subtle, the deep influencing. You transmit or emit energy according to the needs and your judgment of the situation. If you use too much of that energy in that particular situation you may well blow everybody's minds. It doesn't happen, because, fortunately—let me make one thing clear: when I say I monitor the energy it's not because I am a sort of miser and build it up and receive it and keep it round me. The majority of the energy that I have is to be given out. I can't use it personally, and as a matter of fact, I don't want it. Therefore I have to push people to be able to receive it and, as you can see, I cannot say to people: "Ah, how much energy would you like today" and so on ...

There are many different types of energy and different qualities of energy. They are transmitted and received in different ways by different methods, and they are for use in different situations. Not everybody can develop the capacity to use all these different energies, because it is not necessary to be able to use all of them. It is useful, though, to be able to receive all types of them.

In the Tradition, we use a graphic example of how we operate within the Tradition: we call it the oil-spot. Imagine you have a piece of paper and you drop drops of oil separate from each other all over it. Given the correct circumstance, all these drops slowly and gradually and finally will coalesce and cover the whole paper. We call it oil-spot because those drops are drops of energy. The drops of energy spread out, diffuse, and change the character or nature of the paper or the material. Certainly in some places or in some circumstances one wants to accelerate that process, so therefore one puts more drops more closely together.

Those drops of energy have a low profile: they're not getting up and pushing and shouting and shoving. They are creeping and moving and diffusing. They do not provoke a rejection by the paper; there's no battle for control over the paper. It's a natural assimilation. This is one of the ways in which we can and should and do operate in the world today: communication between individuals, between groups, on all levels, by all techniques. Whether you send somebody a postcard, a letter, a bunch of flowers, or marry them—get the contact stronger.

You must always be conscious of the fact that you are members of a great Tradition. This gives you comfort and humility and not arrogance. If you want arrogance, I am a professional. When I say feel that you are in the Tradition, it should be a comfortable and comforting feeling, not a complex: "I am in the Tradition, what should I do now? I have five minutes!" Sit down, relax, do a *zikr*, think of something useful.

I'll just leave you with a saying which is very basic to many of the sayings of the Tradition: "Hold fast to the chain and you will not go astray," and a quote from Rumi which says: "Put your hand into the hand of the Guide; it is better than a light and safer than a known way."

Chapter 15

THE NEED FOR DISCIPLINE

Discipline as a concept and as an instrument; Thinking discipline as opposed to gut-reaction; Flexibility vs. robotic; Quality as opposed to quantity of time; Repetition of objective; Investing in positive activity for the future; Relationship with the external world; Irreplaceability of experience; Willingness to be a cog in a mechanism; Below-normal functioning; Excess energy production.

I have spoken before about the need for, and various aspects of, discipline within the Tradition. Now the word "discipline" itself provokes different reactions and different interpretations to different people. Discipline is a concept and discipline is an instrument. Like every discipline or like every instrument, it can be underused or overused. It is the skill of the person who uses the discipline which changes the character of the discipline.

In the Tradition, discipline is essential. I have a little experience, and I can stand up and shout until you're all deaf and petrified, and you will all stagger out and feel well-disciplined – and you won't understand anything which I have said.

In the Tradition, one must accept the principle of the existence of discipline. Discipline is not only me giving you orders: discipline is also giving yourself orders. Discipline is thinking about things in a correct manner. Discipline should not create robot or mechanical action or thinking. You can have a highly trained soldier, and under a particular battle situation an officer gives him a command: "Go!" If he is a disciplined and a trained soldier, he just doesn't run off in the general direction that officer has indicated.

Before the order has been given he has himself tried to assess the circumstance. When the order is given he puts his discipline into action – he does not just react. This is a thinking discipline, this is not just a gut-reaction. He knows that he is told to go. Now all his training will tell him how to go, whether he should run, whether he should crawl, or whether he should advance slowly.

The officer takes the responsibility for giving the order to that soldier: "Go!" The officer takes the responsibility of observing and controlling the advance of that soldier, but the responsibility of how that soldier goes forward is upon the soldier himself. The officer will not tell him to go forward unless he knows he is sufficiently trained to go forward. If the soldier, despite his training, walks forward slowly and gets his head blown off, the fault is: either the officer has chosen a fool to go forward, or the man has not used his training in going forward. True, you can have a situation where an officer says to a soldier, "Go forward" and, watching him with a microphone shouts, "Yes, a little bit to the right! Mind the man on the left! Climb that wall over there! Keep your head down!" and keep up a constant instruction. This, of course, is impossible and inefficient. Yes, he is controlling the advance of that soldier under the strategic plan which he has, and he will give advice and he will manipulate the other soldiers to help or cover or protect each other.

In training a soldier, you must teach him how to think – how to think in a disciplined fashion. Not in a robot fashion; not in a mechanical fashion. A person has to discipline their own actions and their own thinking. They are very close to themselves – they know their areas of strength and their areas of weakness. They must be honest enough to recognize their weaknesses and try and build up their strengths. Some of these weaknesses may be embarrassing and surprising, and people don't like to admit them, but you cannot hide from yourself. You have to look at yourself – the totality of yourself – and see which areas of yourself or your behaviour need to be improved. This does not mean a constant and critical examination of yourself at all levels. It has to be as much as possible an objective examination – with patience and with understanding, but not with constant excuse.

If you are late for your job, or late for something, you can produce an excuse – and the person may accept it or not – but how can you produce yourself an excuse to give to yourself? Who are you fooling? You say to yourself: "I don't accept that excuse because I made it." The correct discipline and attitude comes in if a person invents an excuse for themselves, and you say, "I'm sorry, I can't accept that excuse."

There is no anger; there is no tension. There is no need for you to shout at yourself: "No!" and in a correct disciplined situation, it should not be necessary for me to shout at you.

If I start shouting in order to make a point very strongly, I assure you that everybody will freeze and their brains will become like jelly, and you will get a little bit of an adrenaline trip. Well I will have strained my vocal cords and nothing will have been achieved. When you're dealing with people who are allegedly intelligent, it is my experience that by the intensity of the voice, by varying the tone of the voice, one can achieve the degree of discipline which is necessary under the circumstance. When one disciplines oneself, one's thoughts, and one's actions, again, this is not a battle – this is not warfare: "Me against myself": the great battle.

You discipline yourself by having a certain list of priorities: things which you wish to achieve, ways in which you want to improve yourself, ways in which you want to improve your professional life or your social life or your living. This list of priorities changes. When one of your priorities on the top of your list is that you have to do an exercise, and number 2 after your exercise is that you have to have something to eat, in some circumstances those priorities will change. If you're so hungry that you can't even think – there is no good doing an exercise. So you eat for physical reinforcement, which enables you to do the exercise, unless of course you have eaten so much and you drink so much that you feel sleepy and you don't do the exercise. Then you end up feeling guilty. So the simple arrangement of that discipline is that you prevent yourself, without a great battle, from eating and drinking too much. You're preparing yourself for step number 2, which is the exercise.

A list of priorities based on a disciplined thinking is not a completely rigid list. A list of things you want to do during the day or during the week should be divided into things that you will try to do, things that you want to do, and things that you must do. If you find that in the category of things you must do are certain exercises – you must work out your other priorities around these fixed points. There is no excuse to avoid the necessity of regular exercise or *zikr*. People say to me sometimes, for one reason or another, "I find it difficult" – "I have a problem in doing the exercise" – either because of "my work" or other time reasons, or otherwise sometimes, "I don't feel that it is right for me to do it." My answer to that is that, as far as I am concerned, neither excuse is good enough. Certainly there may be a fixed schedule – say you want to do an exercise for fifteen minutes in one day. And you look through your programme, and you try and find fifteen minutes, and you try and work it out and you can't find fifteen minutes. Look back over the day before, and see how many minutes, how many periods of one or two minutes you were doing nothing, waiting for something to happen, waiting for somebody to come. I assure you that in that 24 hours, you can find fifteen separate minutes. Certainly a period of fifteen minutes together, yourself – fifteen solid minutes – is better, is more useful, but if you have a very broken-up day, you can still steal from that day times of one or two minutes which put together will be your fifteen minutes.

What makes you look for these minutes is your intention and your discipline. You are looking for opportunities to use your own time best. Time is one thing that does not come back to you. Utilise it to the maximum possible. When you have time, think of time in terms of quality and not of quantity. If you have problems of lack of discipline in your thinking or actions, take yourself under a discipline. If this seems to be so hard, you must repeat to yourself what you are trying to achieve. After all, every time a person puts ten dollars in their savings account, they are thinking about the house, or the apartment, or the car, or the boat, i.e., their intention. This is positive and concrete, something they can imagine. If you're investing your time in activities in the Tradition, you are building up a credit of energy.

I am not promising you or showing you a picture of your place in Paradise, *but I am telling you that man is capable of a development that his imagination cannot comprehend. But he can develop his abilities, he can develop his being to a point where perhaps a seat in Paradise no longer becomes very important.* After all, a seat in Paradise also has its responsibilities. And anyway that is a very fruitful source of other imaginings – "Will it be gold, silver, big, comfortable or not?"

The aim, the intention in the Tradition is in fact a very narrow aim. People start off first in the Tradition with a very large number of thoughts, ideas, hopes, dreams, and other things which they don't quite know about. *And slowly, as they learn and become more accustomed to the Teaching, their aim narrows.* That doesn't mean to say that their enthusiasm becomes any less, it means that some of the things in the beginning which they felt they wanted – gradually they find that they don't really need these things.

It doesn't mean that they "abandon the world" or any comforts, and walk instead of driving a car, or wear sackcloth instead of comfortable clothes – *but it means that they learn that the energy which they can produce and perceive can be used precisely. And every point of internal development reflects on their outside life.* The outside effect is not of a dramatic or startling nature – it is not so much the effect by the person on the outside, it is a modification of their assessment of their position in the world.

Last year when I was in the United States I saw most of our Friends there in the different groups, and one American said to me, "I came into the Tradition two years ago – and when I came in I owed my bank two thousand dollars, and I had no job. Now, after two years, I owe my bank two thousand dollars, and I have no job." So I said to him, "Well, was that a question or a statement?" And he said, "It was a statement." And I said, "Good, thank you for telling me – is there a question?" And he said, "No." So I said, "Well, you should go away, and ask yourself a question: why is it that after two years I still have no job, and after two years I still have no money, and after two years I also have no question?"

In the Tradition, one has to look very carefully when one is looking for what one is calling "results." What is measurably the immediate result of reading or doing an exercise? You do an exercise, you read Hafiz or Jami for a half hour, and then you close the book and you feel if the "winds are going." You may be disappointed to find that they haven't yet appeared, but you have still gained from that reading or that activity.

It is a very common, unfortunately human, desire to do something and then stand back and see what happens. People do it all the time, consciously or unconsciously. If they use the same sort of measurement in the Tradition, it won't work, because you're using a different type of measure. Even after a friend of yours in a group has had a problem for three or four months – if you say to them, "How do you feel?" hopefully they will say, "Well, better." Even if they say, "Not as bad" – it's something. If there was a possibility of, if you like, constant checking of one's development, the human being would spend all his time checking on himself, and if there was no apparent increase in the pulse rate, then they would feel they had lost energy or feel disappointed—and then checking or controlling oneself becomes a constant habit, taking away the energy and dispersing the attention.

You must adhere to a discipline—you must discipline yourselves. I will do the surveying, I will do the pushing, I will do the correcting. As I have said before, I will give you a bicycle, I will teach you to ride it—I will not ride it for you. In the Tradition one must experience oneself. Experiencing oneself is similar to one of our rules, which is "travelling within oneself." Experiencing oneself means measuring or feeling how one feels, what is one's state, in varying circumstances; throughout all the emotions of fear, happiness, sorrow, neurosis; throughout every sort of circumstance—and trying to understand in a simple way how these states can be improved—or else not suppressed, but diminished.

It is not a battle, it is not a war; it is an uphill path. If you climb and stop, and climb and stop—each time restarting requires a little more energy. So it's better that you establish a minimum momentum for climbing, so that each positive activity you do slightly increases the momentum.

There are some times, some occasions and some circumstances, when I might ask a person or a group to increase that momentum. If a group is like a wheel in a clock mechanism, each wheel has a relation to other wheels. It is to the benefit of the whole clock, and it is of benefit to each individual wheel, to work efficiently and together. The mechanism and the wheels of a clock do not work in a democratic fashion. If one wheel decides to go the other way, or to go a little faster, because it feels that it is not its own personality, or whatever rubbish—or it is not sufficiently important—well, then I think that particular wheel should try and participate in or invent a one-wheel clock.

Theoretically, I suppose this is possible: but since the principle of the cog-wheel mechanism is tried and established and exists—why not be a good cog in a good clock? A functioning, equilibriated, balanced, clock does not suffer from psychiatric problems—because, for one thing, if the clock has been put together properly, the balance is controlled by the whole mechanism.

So, in the same way, in a group, the people functioning together, support, compensate and balance the function of each other. There may be moments, for one reason or another, where one member of a group is functioning below normal. It is the function of the group to try and restore the correct functioning of this person by contact and relationship. Equally, it is the function of a group, relating to another group, to try and establish this balancing function. One group may produce an excess amount of energy, which they can store for their own future use, or pass it on to another group, who, at that moment, need an extra boost of energy. Therefore there is the necessity of having as close a rapport as possible between members of groups, and between groups.

Useful energy is not easily produced. There are special situations in which energy can be generated or transmitted between individuals or between groups. These special situations can be used to correct a balance which has become disequilibriated. Such production and transmission of energy from person to person, or from group to group, is not produced by a tension situation. It can and should be produced according to a very careful analysis of the situation. The equation is absolute: efficient thought, put together with correct intention, useful action — must produce developmental progress.

Unfortunately, in Western culture there are many opportunities to indulge in philosophical or intellectual discussion. I am not against philosophy, I am not against intellectual discussion. But I do not like to see activities or writings of the Tradition put in a purely philosophical or purely intellectual context.

When you think about discipline — or when I use the word discipline — understand what I mean about the concept and the application of discipline. If one says, "Right — if my teacher imposes a strong discipline on the group — are we going to then have control of action, control of thought?" No, because I can do that, but I do not call that discipline. I can tell you how to think; I can tell you what to think about. But I cannot and will not do your thinking for you, or put into your minds a little finished, polished and developed thought. I don't need robots, I don't need puppets. I can work with people who can and are prepared to think. If I tell a person to do something, it is for the reason that I have thought about it, that I have thought of the effect and the result. Hopefully, after they do it, they will understand the intention and the benefit of the action.

So discipline in the context of the Tradition is a concept, not a rigid structure of behaviour. There is a slight difference, of course, in army discipline – and if you want army discipline, I can give you hell, and I am very good at it.

But at this particular moment, I want good-thinking groups, and not, for the moment, a good armoured division. Mind you, if, for a reason, I have to change my intention, I won't give you much notice.

Chapter 16

HARMONY AND DISHARMONY

Subjective harmony and disharmony; Inner equivalents to the senses; Understanding and controlling how the negative functions within oneself; Negative and positive patterns; Summoning positive energy; How negativity and positivity work through time; How certain positive efforts pull the negative curve down.

To aspire to achieve harmony, one must learn, take, or touch values. It is harmonious by internal reaction and measurement, and is also harmonious in the more open senses, in the more usual senses, like taste or just ordinary sight.

If you have a tortilla and it smells good, okay, and its colour is red — well, maybe it tastes all right, but some part of you is thinking, "What happened?" or "Why red?" or "Is it different? Let me taste it. It tastes all right, but I am worried because it is red" — and you feel a little unhappy. The same thing happens when a sound or an effect or a colour or speech is being examined or looked at or absorbed by the interior part of a person. The ordinary senses which exist, which you use every day, like taste or touch or smell or listening — if you think of those same values, but much deeper and more refined, much more delicate — that is the equivalent inside, the same thing happens. You have bright red tacos with green spots, and you say, "I am hungry" — you try it, it tastes all right, but you're still not happy about the situation. Your hunger is satisfied because you say, "Well okay, I've tried it, it tastes all right, it smells all right, I eat it and that hunger is satisfied — but still there remains a little question going around, you say, "Well, there must be a reason, because why that colour?" and one part of you is satisfied because your hunger is satisfied, but this creates a question or a confusion about the colour. You don't want to go about for days or weeks or months wondering about why was this taco green?

A similar thing happens with the interior being of a person. It gets the nourishment, it gets the energy, and if that nourishment or that energy has been sent correctly or been generated correctly, then there is no question or doubt about the colour of this energy. Because if the nourishment or the energy is sent, received and used correctly, the receiving part of the person says, "Right, I got the energy, I used it correctly – the question of its colour is not important."

The measurement is: if you can use that energy correctly, then you can get it. If you get too much, you use some and you have some left – this can cause you a problem because you say, "What shall I do with this?" or "Should I have used all the energy which I received on that thing, instead of having some remaining?" Now this in fact doesn't happen. And there is a third point: you can say, "Now I have some energy left, I must be careful not to use it in a stupid way."

Well, firstly, if it is proper, deep, energy – you can't waste it, you can't use it on something stupid. You receive the energy you produce yourself, as well as the energy that you get from the group, and the energy from the Tradition. You get the correct amount – the amount that you can use and that you have the ability to use.

Now this is quite natural, because very refined energy should not be given to people who can't use it properly. Not that they can use it stupidly, because if they have too much, and they hold it for only two minutes, it is almost a waste of that energy, because it doesn't become used – yet it could be used more efficiently in those two minutes by somebody else or by another group. So the time it takes for your inner being to find out that it has this much more, and the time it takes – maybe two seconds or one second – to get that back to the store where it can be sent out again – is a waste of one second. So you get enough quantity so that that one second is saved – it's not wasted. You don't get into the situation or question: Did I use enough? What should I do with this? – and everything else.

Now in all situations of the Tradition, you find that they are based on balance and harmony. This is necessary – it is also efficient – because some people by nature are more active or energetic than others. Some people act in a spontaneous way – some people think more before they do something. All of these attitudes are correct, providing, again, you have balance. If you say, "All right, I will think for half an

hour whether I shall put milk in my coffee or not" — you get cold coffee. If you say, "Right, there is coffee, sugar, milk, and a cup: and you
put it all in and you drink it all spontaneously, because it's there, and
you think: "Ah, I don't like milk in my coffee" — one person is feeling
terrible because they used everything spontaneously — and the other
person is feeling terrible, because they got a terrible cup of coffee.

The balance you have with colour, with shape, with form is something you see in nature. If you saw a tree, and it was growing chrysan-
themums — then you would think that is a bit strange — something funny.
For instance, when talking of certain functional parts of the body: the
heart, the lungs, the liver, and so forth, which have a specific function.
If any of those are not working correctly in the sense that they are not
doing their job, that can cause a temporary imbalance.

Another reason why an imbalance can happen is that people say:
"Ha, I do something positive, I do an exercise, I do a *zikr*, and somehow maybe I don't feel so good or I feel something." And sometimes
they say, "Ah, it's because I did that wrong" or "I did that at the wrong
time" — now this is possible, but it doesn't happen very often. If that is
not the reason, and if not some temporary physical disturbance — what
is it? It is coming from the negative.

It is important for us, in the Tradition, to understand — especially
for the people who have joined us newly — that when I use the term
"your negative part" or "it comes from somewhere negative in you" —
what precisely do I mean? So you say, "No, no, don't worry, because we
understand, have been told or have read that there is the negative and
the positive personality — sometimes I am controlled by my positive personality and sometimes by my negative personality." This is rubbish. It
is invented by psychologists or psychiatrists because "the schizophrenic
battle between my positive being and my negative being — and to find
how I can think positively and control this negative side of me" — takes
a long time, and, at a hundred dollars an hour, it costs a lot of money,
so it's a good business.

The actual fact is this: because of negative contacts, negative experiences, and various negative influences, a person takes on a certain
quantity of negative charge in a lifetime. *But remember this, and remember this carefully — the negative — if you want to measure it — is much
smaller and much weaker than the positive.* The negative acts in a way

which causes temporary confusion, doubt, complication, even physical pain. *The positive, using positive energy, produces effects which are deep and clear and permanent and capable of being passed on through the generations.* The negative part is fighting, in fact, for survival. If your thoughts, your actions and the energy you use is positive, you can diminish the influence of the negative part over you so much that it will use every opportunity to show itself.

But its quality is like that of a stinging mosquito's technique: it bites you here, you scratch it; it bites you there, you scratch it—thinking, "Damn, these mosquitos!" It is occupying your thoughts, occupying your energies, so sometimes you don't think—you don't stop for a moment and think: "Maybe I should close the window" or "Maybe I should put on some anti-mosquito ointment" because it's got you reacting: it hasn't got you thinking. It must do this as much as possible. Why? Because it can't take you over completely, and it knows that, but if you are using it in everything you do, you are pushing that negative into a corner, and it has nowhere to go. Nobody wants to take it from you— they say, "Thank you very much, I have enough problems." To act against the negative, you find out how it operates within you: in your character, in your actions. Once you start seeing the way it operates in you and in other people, you can recognize it in operation.

Now that is more than half the battle, because there are many possibilities of what you then do against it. That is why I say that identifying it clearly is more than half the battle. People react in a negative way"—they think in a negative way—nearly always according to a particular pattern. If you can look at a situation after it has happened, and, a minute before it starts—if you look at the activity which has happened—and you look at it carefully, calmly, not immediately after you have come out of it, and you're still tensed up—you look at it: now "What went wrong? Where did I go wrong? Where did the situation go wrong? Where did somebody do something which caused me to react in a negative way?

If you do this every time something happens, not only with the negative occasions, but also with the positive and useful occasions—when you've studied a few of them, you should begin to see the pattern of negative and the pattern of positive. In this way, among other ways, you get a clearer picture of yourself. You can say to yourself: "Right, my

negative or weak points are in this sort of area." Equally, "My strong
or positive points are in this area of activity." You can't always say,
"Right, I will use those activities or look for solutions only where I can
use the positive, and any situation or contact which is in the negative
area within me, I will avoid."

Obviously you can't always do that. It's not always possible to avoid
a situation which you don't like. It is not always possible to enter only
situations which you like and you know that you can make positive.
Sometimes you can avoid the negative ones, or the ones leading to a
negative result – sometimes you can do it. So what do you do when you
seem to be drawn to a situation which you are almost sure is going to
be negative? Firstly you must be careful that there is the possibility of
negative coming or arising out of that situation – and it's not that you
have already decided that it's going to be negative. "It's Friday the thirteenth, and I saw a black cat, and you know, I'd better stay at home." If
it is not just imagination – before you go into the situation, put yourself
in contact with, call upon, summon up, and *take the positive into that
situation with you. This has two effects: if the negative influence in that
is little enough, the amount of positive energy which you take in can change
that situation into a positive one.*

If the situation is very strongly negative, and you can't take enough
positive in to change it, then at least use that positive energy which you
have taken in to protect yourself against the negative in that situation.
You use it to look at the situation, and to see how the negative operated
in that situation – did it operate through somebody? Did it operate
through some subject under discussion? Did it operate because of the
ambiance, the place where you were or was the situation that you were
actually physically in negative, in the sense that it was maybe cold or
maybe uncomfortable, maybe somehow hostile?

This is the operation of the so-called negative and positive personalities. One might say, "Well, if the positive part is stronger and bigger, why doesn't it just destroy the negative? It is a gradual tactic which
you use – you don't want to provoke one big battle inside yourself, because it's not necessary. You have a series of continual little battles –
you don't lose much positive energy in those battles. Each time you use
it, each time you're successful, you know better and more precisely how
to use it, and you learn to feel the satisfaction of achieving a positive

result, because you say to yourself: "I used positive energy. Some of it I generated myself, some I got from the group, some I got from the reserve of the Tradition – but I used it. I used it correctly, and I got the positive result." "Oh, I can't do it because I'm so stupid or so weak" or "I am alone" or "I am Argentine" or some other excuse – or else, "All right, I'll try it and something will help me" – something will help you, certainly. The positive energy which you can call upon and which, again, you learn to use.

If Miguel is hungry and I eat his breakfast, he doesn't get the satisfaction of the breakfast. He loses a little experience in how to eat breakfasts. If you go to a doctor and you say: "I have a sore throat," and he says, "Yes, you have a sore throat" and he gives himself a penicillin injection, this doesn't help you much. You can say, "This is marvelous, but I wish he had given it to me."

You can do it: it is there to be used. *Because the function of the Tradition is to exist among people and to reawaken in them the capacity to use themselves correctly.* In the Tradition, we don't want puppets. We want to show and teach people how to think and how to act, by developing themselves and feeling their own increasing capacity – with the help of energy, with the help of guidance – knowing that putting their intention, energy, and direction together to do something – believing that it works – and makes it work.

These tactics are not just to be remembered and thought about. They are to stimulate action and to become an accepted part of your nature and behaviour. They have to be accepted by you, after you have thought about them and considered them, because if you do not accept them freely they become another form of conditioning.

People are conditioned from the time they are babies – socially, economically, politically, religiously, and in every possible way. They grow up in a society which is similarly affected. Eighty percent of the conditioning which they have received as they grow up comes out in their behaviour and their attitude: "We Mexicans are like this" – "We French are like this" – "We this are like that." Not all this conditioning is bad – if it is a conditioning which helps you in life, then, whether it is called conditioning or experience, it is still valuable. But if it is a conditioning which tells you what to think and how to react, it can be dangerous because it can ignore what you might like to call "internal feeling" or instinct. If you are a product of a certain form of intellectual or religious conditioning, perhaps it is difficult to say: "I don't completely accept this." In a religious sense, people may say, "You are unbelievers, you are outside the Church, you have no faith." In an intellectual sense, if you say: "I don't understand Schopenhauer" — possibly people will measure you according to that statement, and they might say, "He's not intellectual; he hasn't read Schopenhauer."

In society, you must have certain fixed measures and rules of behaviour. One can agree on a measure of distance or weight, on a measure of heat or cold, on techniques in chemistry, mathematics or physics — these you must have, because, as you can imagine, if everybody had a different measurement which they used, there would be chaos. Okay — so everybody agrees on certain things. It is when you get into what we call in the Tradition, the profounder, deeper self, that you have to be careful that the conditioning of the world does not affect that inner being.

If you use conventional measurements or conventional terms to measure internal capacity or development — in other words, if you use conventional expressions or terms to express deep feelings, there can be problems. If you want to express a feeling when you have a deep spiritual reaction to something, you can say to some other person in the Tradition, "I read such-and-such a thing," or "I visited such-and-such a place and I felt something." If you share an experience you don't have to explain it. It is not that you are being imprecise, it is a question of how do you express, in conventional terms, what you felt? In terms of quantity, in terms of quality, in terms of depth? You can't. You don't need to.

I'm not saying that you shouldn't try. What I am saying is that an experience that two people or a number of people may share, let's say that it may cause them to cry. Now conventionally measured, people cry because they're alone, because they're afraid, because they are hurt, because they are sad — also they can cry with joy. You say to a person, "I went to Granada and it hit me." If they have been, they will probably say to you, "Yes, I know the feeling." They are not going to examine you like a doctor: "Was it your feet which hurt, did you feel sick? Did you get a temperature?" — because this is a deep experience.

What am I talking about? I'm talking about a shared experience or a shared impact which has an effect, and, at the same time, establishes a communication between you. If you like, it's a new language. It cuts down the necessity of putting into words things which cannot be put into words or which are unnecessary to put into words.

In every activity of the Tradition, you are encouraged to experience circumstances and impacts produced as a group in an activity, and the energy which you draw from the Tradition. By using the techniques, by adding the energy, you have the experience. Much can be written and thought and discussed theoretically. You can have people who are good speakers and who are good writers, who, as they say, "With their words, they paint a picture." Can anybody with a good descriptive capacity and vocabulary, who can write descriptively and well, explain to me, or write me a paragraph, so that I can appreciate the taste of an onion? You can get near it — you can describe the texture, the colour, the shape, you can describe its use in cooking, you can describe how it cured your grandmother's bronchitis — that doesn't tell me anything.

You say, well, why the analogy of a simple thing like that? Because if it is not possible to do it with an onion, which is a simple thing — how can you do it with a spiritual experience, which is ten thousand times more difficult to describe? In the Tradition you find a slightly different type of technique — how to grow an onion, how to cultivate an onion correctly, what you can use an onion for. And then it tells you: Do it! Eat it! When you have done these things correctly, the concept of what is an onion is complete. So in the Tradition we teach how, when, where, and also why.

The Tradition is essentially and basically an active technique. It is not a detrimental and self-sabotaging acceptance of fate. This is an excuse. You have every opportunity, every capacity, every ability, every assistance, every technique available — don't tell me that you can sit here and become or not become, or affect or not affect. If God had created man to remain a cabbage, why should He have created a cabbage with a capacity? You show me somebody who lies on their back all day like Nasrudin under an apple tree, thinking, "If it's God's will, an apple will fall into my mouth!" — and I will show you a lazy ignorant fool.

Okay — so I'm not very charitable towards people's lack of responsibility towards themselves. No, I'm not: I have no patience with them, I have neither my time nor their time to waste.

There is energy, there is technique, there is capacity, there is need, there is opportunity — with all those things, you do not cook a pot of soup, you use them. *You use the potential.* If I get angry, if I am impatient with some people, it is because I am angry at what they are not doing for themselves. I may show impatience because they are slow in realizing how they can develop. Some people, perhaps many people, find me opinionated, lacking in sympathy or kindness and call me dictatorial or megalomaniac. All these may be true, probably, except one, and that is the megalomaniac one, because by definition, a megalomaniac wants and tries to get possession, to possess and control everything. So how can I be a real megalomaniac?

I have yet to discover that I suffer from megalomania. Megalomania is time-consuming and if it doesn't work, gradually your megalomania diminishes, and the result is just disappointment. So maybe I could be permitted to be a little megalomaniac. But that does not prevent me from watching all of you — not for signs of megalomania, which are obvious — but watching you for a lack of efficient use of the instruments and the techniques of the Tradition. If you want problems with me, ignore the techniques, the instruments, and the energy of the Tradition. I won't discuss it with you, I won't negotiate with you; I will explain to you, I will push you, I will pull you, and do almost any other unpleasant thing you can think of — providing that under the circumstances, it produces the necessary positive effect.

Don't ask me or expect me to come in and out on a magic carpet. Don't expect me to teach you how to fly a magic carpet, because, strangely enough, I want people to listen to me, study and work, because I don't use a magic carpet. You can float about Mexico for a couple of days on a magic carpet and you'll get a million people wanting to know where they can get one, how they can fly it. If you tell them, "It takes a long time, a lot of doing, a lot of discipline, a lot of listening to me" — you get rid of ninety percent of them almost immediately. So I hope you are here, basically, because I haven't got a magic carpet.

Chapter 17

POSITIVITY VERSUS NEGATIVITY

Importance of basic values; Conflicts between peoples, countries, societies and within oneself; Activating energy over time; Build-up of negative and positive energies; How tension situations build up.

Wars occur in which millions die.

The reason is this: that there are periods in the history of each planet when certain basic values, certain important things, are not popular — they are thought "unnecessary," or "not modern," or for some other reason they can be conveniently ignored. Those things which people ignore or put to one side can be the positive things. People say: "Look, a positive attitude is to say, all right, you want this piece of territory, I want this piece of territory — if we fight over this territory, what have we learnt in five million years?"

Five million years ago, one man wanted that bone and the other man also wanted that bone, so one killed the other — all right. And one of them got it — he was happy, he'd killed somebody else, no matter. So what did humanity learn? It learnt, theoretically, that if you explode an atom bomb and you kill eighty thousand people — in theory. And they all say, "All right, we won't do it — until it is useful or convenient for us to do it — okay."

There are periods in the existence of each planet where the positive energy is there, and there is enough positive energy which could stop a war, stop people thinking about a war, stop people needing a war. Sometimes that energy does not activate itself, does not have a hundred percent effect on the situation — that is, to stop a war — and the reason is that if you take a time-scale from 0 to 9000 years — from this point and from different points in world time, in planetary time, there are people who attract energy, develop energy. Some of it, which they use locally, is transmitted to surface at a particular time, at a particular place — and this goes on constantly.

You say, "Okay, now this is 1940." Now by a complicated method, if you are the source which is sending this energy to 1940, you can predict that there will be a certain degree of negative at that time. Sometimes it is possible to work out exactly how much negative there will be, and sometimes an amount of positive energy is sent to be released at that time—much smaller, because of the relation: one degree of positive equals ten degrees of negative. So if the information and prediction is right, then that will cancel this out, and no bigger negative situation will happen. Sometimes it happens that the amount of energy which is available to be sent to that particular place is smaller, is less, and it's not sufficient to cancel out the negative which is generated. Okay, now you might say, "Right, now if it is possible over a period of time, to measure particular quantities of negative energy which can be more or less predicted—why not send approximately enough, or even more, to make sure?"

There are two reasons for this.

The first is possibly that the time period here which is responsible for sending energy for this other time period, doesn't have enough energy to completely cancel out the negative—so it sends out as much as possible to limit the amount of damage, if you like, because it may be a point out of which two or three other future times of tension are being supplied.

This is where mankind comes into the picture, because if this amount of negativity exists at that time-period—as I say, at 1940—you cannot say that that negative energy has suddenly arrived from somewhere. It has been built up by mankind. Until 1940, the build-up had been regular, until it reaches a point where it can no longer be contained, and it explodes. And then the same situation happens over and over again. So you say, "Well then, is this the fate of humanity?—to threaten itself, damage itself, destroy itself every so many years or so many time-periods?" No, because if this were a predictable graph—number of years: negative energy building up and then you get, you know the famous graph syndrome: it goes up and down, and it would be constantly repetitive.

If it really was like that, you could confidently predict in 19 something, I had better take a boat and row out into the Atlantic. But the graph is not regular—it is peak, peak, and nothing. Now what happens when the graph, instead of going up in tension or negative energy – why does it either go less steeply, or what happens when it completely flattens out and goes for some centuries without a big peak of negativity? It is because between point x and 1940 the graph was going constantly up, because the people and the civilizations through which it was passing were each supporting, by their thoughts and their action, the increase in tension. In times when the graph is flat, or goes down, it is because the people or the civilizations or the communities in that time period are not supporting this tension increase, but are pulling it down from the upwards curve. They have the knowledge, they have the techniques, they have the desire for peace rather than war. Sometimes they are successful in keeping the curve down – sometimes they are successful in pulling it right down.

The flat line, or the downward path of the line, shows how much the people, the civilizations and the communities in that period of the line being flat – how much effort and how much use they have made of the knowledge, the material, and techniques which they have to mobilize to keep that line straight. You can see it, it's perfectly clear. When it goes right down: that is a time-period of a civilization or a people or a community really pulling it down through effort.

You see, to develop people, you not only develop within them capacities, techniques, give them knowledge and teach them how to use them – you have to leave it to them to have the desire to learn and to use these techniques. You might say "This is cruel" because it is possible to reinforce these lines of energy, and influence the thinking, the desires and the needs of the people – we can have a constant flat line or we can have a constant line going down – so surely this is playing with people's lives, this is playing with civilization? It is not, because humanity must make, and desire to make, the effort. They have the technique, they have the knowledge, they have the ability, they have the guidance, they have the possibility of generating the energy – they don't use it.

You might say, "Well, do they deserve to be protected from themselves? Should their impatience, greed, negativity, be excused, ignored or accepted as natural, so that when they have built it up to a dangerous degree, somebody or some people can remove the negativity, and life goes on normally, and mankind has not learnt that he has been saved?"

You can over-protect, until you get a general social and psychological attitude that something will happen. "No problems – something will happen." You can produce generations and civilizations and societies of irresponsible puppets – where their desire or feeling for development is ignored, where they lose contact with the cosmos or nature who are telling them "Watch it" or "Watch out" – or else they say, "We are strong enough to survive anything." This is more or less the situation that you have now in this time-period.

You have basically two great forces – and as one gets a little stronger, so the other must keep pace with the other. In a situation like that, something must happen – not necessarily a war, but a long period when people, their families, their children, live in a state of tension – where more and more money, effort, energy, is spent on getting stronger and stronger to match the other one – and the whole thinking and economy and attitude of the people changes. It changes in many ways: in one way it changes because people looking at their strength, say, feel confident. They are encouraged to think in that way until it becomes a normal and natural way of thinking. This is not normal, this is not natural – because if you have a nuclear war in three years' time or in five years' time, leaving aside the horror and death and suffering of millions of people, the period between that nuclear explosion and the beginning of the tension in civilization – you have learnt nothing. So you say, "Well, we have learned: I don't want to be bombed; I don't want to see a nuclear war; we have learned what the horror of nuclear war is" – of course we have learned, but you haven't learnt the technique of preventing this build-up of tension.

This world-situation of a build-up in tension is the same as the build-up of tension in a person – they build up the tension, they don't think clearly that they have this tension; they don't understand how they can get rid of this tension – because if it goes on long enough, they will say, "Well, I'm like that." When the tension builds up too much, they go out and break a window or punch a policeman or do something. They've got rid of that tension – coincidentally they have gone to jail or something as a result of that. They're not happy about going to jail, but they say, "But I understand, it was logical, I did something violent, I went to jail."

This is cause and effect. The cause is the tension, the effect is breaking the window, the result is going to jail—so to them, the picture is complete. Until the next time they build up the tension and they go out and they punch a policeman or they break a window and they go to jail. So it's another complete circle. If they build up the tension and go out and beat their mother-in-law—depending on the size of mother-in-law, they either get beaten up themselves, or the wife and the mother-in-law join together and beat him up, and he goes home with a black eye, torn to pieces, bleeding and everything like that—but at least he's learnt something. Now before anybody says, "The way to learn is to go and beat up your mother-in-law because I said so"—don't try it, or if you try it, don't say I told you.

You have a build-up, a climax—the fellow gets beaten: this time it's not jail so maybe it's not so bad, depending on how badly he's got hurt, but at least he—unless he is absolutely stupid—he thinks, "You know, beating up mothers-in-law is not a good idea"—okay. So at least it's one positive thought or one positive lesson he's got. With that piece of learning, the tension has built up and he goes out and he finds somebody smaller than he and he beats them up and he goes home—this is not a very desirable activity, but at least he's learned another little lesson. Say he spends his whole life like that—doing things which are successful or which aren't successful—and from that lack of success he learns to succeed next time, and he sort of goes up and down, sometimes winning, sometimes losing, sometimes getting beaten up—and each time he is getting a fragment of information. By these positive and negative experiences he learns a certain amount, but he doesn't really learn enough.

So, as they lower his coffin into the grave, you hear him knocking on it and saying, "I haven't finished my experiences yet!"

Why doesn't he do something much simpler? Why doesn't he realize that there are some things which must be experienced, and some things which can be learned from the experience of others. Without hesitation he accepts the existence of the radio, the airplane, the motor car, which are the results of other people's work, research and effort left for his benefit. He never thinks, "I want to listen to Radio Madrid, therefore I will make a radio—and after I have listened to it, then I will destroy the radio, and the next time I want to hear it I will build another one," because he knows that with a certain amount of effort he can get a certain amount of money, go to a place, pay the money, buy a radio.

Some people insist that certain things must be experienced personally. This is absolutely correct, but you don't experience them personally in a sort of random way. They experience them correctly when they have read a certain amount, or profited a certain amount from other people's teaching and wisdom, and a point comes when a personal experience of a certain nature is necessary. So that's really it: the taking advantage of a teaching, advice, wisdom, techniques – and, at times, when they are prepared or when it is necessary for them, to experience a particular experience, a particular taste, a particular sensation – that it may be possible for them to experience and understand. As I say, the experiencing, the doing, and what you might call the theoretical side – go along together.

Now if they are following the teaching or wisdom – and they find that experience, that sensation, that taste, they will be able to use it – within the context of the discipline they are following. You have people who say, "Experience, fine – I'll try anything once." So you say, "Right, try potassium cyanide" – "Go and have the experience of catching a rattlesnake" – and that will certainly be a very profound experience and, if the person survives, they are a little bit wiser.

Chapter 18

Contact as a communication instrument within the Tradition; Discipline, belief and faith; Role and danger of preconceived notions; Importance of uncluttered communication-lines; Attitudes about money; The Tradition as an update of past teaching; Flexibility of techniques in the Tradition.

When you have contact by letter, this is efficient only if you know the person and you know what effect the letter is going to have on them. In the Tradition, you have to put a face to a name: the name must mean something in terms of the face, and in terms of a being, an existence.

This point of view of function of making people understand, is to make them understand. If you have, which you should have, different ways of communicating, you must choose the most efficient way of communication for the person or the circumstance.

There are different forms of contact — a contact is not limited by geographical or distance considerations. If an actual physical contact is required, then it can be made. If a contact of equal value can be made by another technique which does not require travel, then let it be done. None of you should ever feel out of contact — out of physical contact, in a sense yes — out of sight, from the point of view of sight, yes — but not out of contact. You are as close to me and to the Tradition as you want to be — or as far from me and the Tradition as you want to be. The Tradition exists for people and with people. It is not a one-way traffic. It is a two-way traffic, a two-way contact, in that the Tradition works in and with people, there is a human aspect to it. It is not a cold, calculated, domination of people. It is possible to confuse discipline with terror. The two do not and cannot live together, and as far as I am involved in any aspect of the Tradition, I will not permit or help in any aspect of rigid control of people's lives.

Discipline? — Essential. Belief and faith? — Essential. These things are imposed both by the teacher on the person, and also by the person on themselves. I can take any person or any group and shout at them for an hour, and get them thoroughly confused, and they will do anything, believe anything, think anything — for a time. For a short time. When the effect of that shouting and menace wears off, then I have to shout again. So we're not getting teaching or understanding, what we're getting is a sort of kangaroo race. It may look very exciting, it may pump a lot of adrenaline into the blood, but I am afraid that it achieves nothing in the real sense. Some of you have first-hand experience of this type of activity. Some people that we know are still experiencing this. Now this concerns me a bit — it concerns me, because in many cases it was done in my name or in the name of the Tradition.

I have had letters from people concerning this, and some of them have asked me what they can do and why I don't stop this. The answer is clear: everything takes a minimum time, whether it's boiling an egg or building a house. You might say, "Yes, but what about the damage which is being done during this time?" The answer to that is that there is no damage which is my concern. That is not to say that I am indifferent to this circumstance — I am concerned about damage which is deep. Discomfort, near-slavery, is, of course, uncomfortable — and I would not wish it to happen — certainly not in my name or in the name of the Tradition. The humiliation of people is inefficient and unproductive — so if it is not productive, why have it?

Just as I have to know you, you also have to get a little bit accustomed to me and my attitude. I'll give you an example why — a very simple example. Somebody phoned me from Berlin, and we had a conversation about the situation and various aspects of the Tradition. This person had not met me and didn't know me — they'd only heard about me — and we had a fairly average conversation about certain aspects of the Tradition and their relation with it. So, two or three days later I received a letter from the husband of this girl in which he said, "My wife had a conversation with you two or three days ago, and you were very cold and almost hostile." If she didn't know me — she'd never met me — how does she know how I sound when I'm cold and hostile? From the context of what I said — there were not cold or hostile words then — so they made this decision that I was cold and hostile, and they were very unhappy. This is understandable — they were asking for my help, so if in reply I am cold and hostile, they have reason to be unhappy — because I wasn't cold and hostile. The reason I quote this example is to show the fact that if they had known better, they would have known, for example, that the angrier I am, the lower my voice. Well, normally my voice is fairly low—but I mean for example, if I start whispering then get out of the room.

If you have in your mind an image of somebody and a preconceived idea, then you really don't need to make that telephone call. You have already decided that the person is cold and hostile, so maybe you're making the telephone call just to confirm this fact. There is a Nasrudin story which describes this situation exactly. In fact, there usually is a Nasrudin story which describes every situation exactly.

Nasrudin wanted to borrow a sickle for cutting wheat. He didn't have one, so he thought he'd borrow one from his neighbour. His neighbour lived about two kilometres away, and Nasrudin thought, "It's a nice day, I'll walk over and borrow the sickle." So as he was walking along, he thought, "You know, I haven't seen this fellow for a long time, I don't really know him very well." He walked along for a bit, and he thought, "What will he think if I suddenly appear and ask if I can borrow the sickle?" And he walked along a little bit more, and said, "He is a bit of a nasty fellow," and he walked along a bit more, and he said to himself, "He's also very mean," and he walked along further, and he said, "You know, he's not going to lend me this sickle. He's going to laugh at me and abuse me, and slam the door." So he went up to the neighbour's door and knocked, and the neighbour opened the door, and said, "Good morning, Nasrudin," and Nasrudin said to him: "Don't you give me all that false politeness—I don't want your damned sickle!" and he went off.

That is an example of what is called a preconceived attitude. I'm not blaming the people for their analysis of that telephone call, I wrote them quite a strong letter in reply and I think I probably frightened them. I would ask you all to be in contact — not that you telephone each other every hour to see if you're still alive or anything like that, but so that people get fairly familiar with each other and can and might pass through and visit or something like that—without it being a sort of a great traumatic experience.

Admittedly when you do meet, you will naturally be likely to discuss certain aspects of the Tradition. That doesn't mean to say that you discuss only the Tradition. You can discuss, compare notes if you like, but don't compare or share activities or exercises, unless it happens that you are both meeting on the same evening and therefore you can participate in that meeting.

There will be some circumstances in which I will delegate authority to a person in a group to act on my behalf. As far as is possible, the members of the group will be informed of this by me. Of course there may be circumstances that I will communicate with somebody in a group and say: "Would you kindly tell the others this or that?" – so that is not to say that if anybody says, "Omar Ali-Shah asked me to tell you this," that you view him all with terrible suspicion. This is where you must have confidence and trust among yourselves, and also I will be keeping a close check on this form of transmission or contact, and a person in the group can possibly get away with it once.

As I was saying, we want to get back onto a positive and functional road. Ordinary life itself has enough complications without introducing other unnecessary ones. The techniques which I will introduce will not be unfamiliar to you – they'll possibly be slightly different in terms of length, or the addition or subtraction of music or some other thing. They will require, again, two forms of discipline. One is the discipline which I ask from you, and the other is the discipline which you impose on yourself. From your point of view, the second discipline is the most difficult. Don't forget that the activities, the techniques of the Tradition help you to develop this discipline.

You are not alone in disciplining yourself – it is not a battle against yourself. You're not tearing yourself apart – you are using functionally useful tools, if you like. Knowing how to use those tools gives you the ability to use them, and the better you know, the more familiar these tools are to you, the more opportunities you find of using them. You know, a hammer is as efficient or inefficient as you use it. It is you who impose limitations on that hammer. The nature of the hammer is unlimited – you can use it "only for cracking nuts" and if you want to put a nail in, and then you call somebody from outside with equipment to put a nail in – you didn't change the character of that hammer. So the hammer is as good or bad as you care to make it. You don't change the nature of an object or a circumstance – it is the use that it is put to which is important.

What is the nature or quality of water? A thirsty man in the desert dreams of it. A drowning man doesn't need it. So its nature is influenced – not changed, influenced – by the circumstance. So, similarly, with exercises or readings. At a particular time or in a particular circumstance, a particular exercise or a particular piece of reading, done or read at the wrong time, can create not damage – but confusion. And the smallest positive thing at the right time, has enormous value. So what do you do, how do you know when is the right moment? You don't have a time-table: "Tuesday, the second of November, at three-thirty will be a good moment, therefore I'd better be ready for it." These correct times or moments do exist and they are predictable – part of my function is to watch this time-scale concerning individuals and groups, and to make sure that they either have the contact or the information that they're going to need at that time.

Part of the activities are to give a person a feel for times or situations, so that by a combination of circumstances, they find themselves doing or participating in an activity which makes them feel good, and which feels right to them. They are developing, in fact, a feel – a touch. That is not to say that they should be sitting on their own shoulder watching themselves for the "right moment" or trying to feel themselves whether this is the right moment to do this or that – because this is a very time-consuming thing, and it doesn't really give you any time to do things like earn your living, and things like that – so usually, you starve.

A lot has been said about money or earning a living. Now there are certain attitudes gloating around concerning, as I say, money and earning a living. Every person, by background, conditioning and other things has their own attitude towards money, its value and importance and so forth. Money is not by definition a dirty thing. It has its correct place in life. It is a fuel, like gasoline. One works, one earns it, one uses it to dress oneself, to eat, to make oneself comfortable. Money should be a thing which one earns and one uses – it only becomes a dominating factor if it becomes the aim of life. One needs, obviously, a certain amount to pay the gas, the electricity, etc., and there's no harm at all in earning a little bit more than what one needs – this is not an abominable and a sinful thing to do. If one wants to earn a little bit more than one needs, and either save it or use it to increase one's own knowledge, comfort, wardrobe — this is not terrible as long as the correct proportion of effort is used to get this money.

Everybody can starve in a garret with no heat and no furniture, and by starving themselves to death, prove that it is possible to starve oneself to death. Poverty does not automatically confer some sort of development. To justify the attitude that money is dirty and that work is unnecessary, people use the examples of some teachers or Saints or people of the past.

As far as I and the Tradition are concerned, there is a total, complete and known and rigid *Silsila* — the line of teaching. There are known teachers, the known guides, the known hierarchy, and there is no room in this *Silsila* for any more prophets. All the places are taken. Anyone can declare himself and feel himself and be, to a degree, a teacher, a guide, somebody who explains things, but our hierarchy, our *Silsila*, the transmission of the *Baraka*, is established to the degree that there are and there will be none other than those who adhere to the particular *Silsila* and the particular transmission of the *Baraka*. People can and do, as I say, declare themselves to be Qutubs, Sheikhs, anything in the world — it is their problem. You know the old saying that "A patched cloak doesn't mean that the man is a Dervish."

As far as we're concerned in the Tradition, there are in the sayings and the writings of the great ones, indications — both in time and in area — where individuals or groups will develop a certain quality of activity which may spread or broaden the influence of a past teacher of the fourteenth or thirteenth century. Present-day or future teachers or guides will update the techniques, not the basic teaching. They project it according to the needs and the facilities, technical or otherwise, or the circumstance — and the influence of the *Silsila*, of the descent, of the hierarchy, is felt all the time and is manifested all the time, in the shape of the *Baraka* and in the shape of the writings and information which they left.

It is up to us to use, take advantage, and benefit from that information and Baraka without going through the sort of birth-pains all over again. Now we do that all the time, as a matter of course, as a normal thing. If you want to go from one place to another, you don't sit down and invent a motor car and then build one — there are things called taxis, so you use that. It's not a great thing for you: "No, it's not the same if I had invented it, it would have been better" — no.

For instance, you have a very good example: a few years ago, a man, Rafael Lefort, wrote a book called *The Teachers of Gurdjieff* in which he described a journey, a search. A lot of people think mistakenly that they should also do the same journey — well, if they have the time, the money and so on, certainly — it's not destructive, it's not wrong. But the information in that book, his discussions or conversations with people are useful, valuable, fairly competent, and if a person says, "Ah, in Istanbul, or Konya, or X or Y, there is a centre of teaching, I will go there and I will try and speak to a Sheikh or a teacher" — he may very well have the same conversation as Lefort had with the same person or his successor or his companion. He may feel happier because it's rewarding — he has made the journey, and he has suffered, and he has got an information.

But instead of using that energy to go and find or confirm that information, why not take that information and put it together with the energy which you would use to go to Istanbul and come back and use it — that is, harness that energy to the information of the energy?

You see the idea: that there is a certain conditioned ethic that somehow suffering brings a reward, or suffering is a reward in itself. This may be all right if one is a masochist; or, if a person is so deeply conditioned that they must suffer to learn; or unless they have suffered they don't think they have learned — then by all means let them go through a period of suffering, if it produces something useful or positive. If it's suffering for suffering's sake, then as I say, it is a useless indulgence. Because I assure you, I am capable of it — I once was very kind to a group of people — it was about a year ago — there were quite a number of people, and I had a table, a tape recorder, and four bottles of whisky. And in the course of a two-hour talk, I drank all four bottles.

Everybody was very impressed, they thought this had a function, and after the meeting most of them went out and tried to do the same thing. Except there was only one difference — that my whisky was cold tea. The reason for that was not really to demonstrate anything other than the fact that, inevitably, somebody who is in a teaching relationship with other people — to a certain degree and in certain ways, the person is emulated, that person is copied. Now this is very right and proper, providing that the things that they copy are useful and functional things. So that was the context of my discussion with them on that night, and yet a number of them made a mental or other note that, you know, "Four bottles of whisky in two hours must be good," and as I say they went out and tried to do it. But it was four bottles — not four bottles of whisky. As you know well the morning after.

As far as contact or communication are concerned, if there are questions, if there are areas of confusion in the air, if you feel that something valuable could be served by writing to me or telephoning to me, do so. I won't judge you or measure you by the number of letters or the length of your telephone calls — or absence of them, either — but I would rather the person would write to ask something which really concerns them, rather than that they should stumble around it themselves and probably come up with the wrong answer.

And one thing which, please, you will get rid of, psychologically and physically, is anything which has any relationship with fear. Never confuse discipline with fear. If I shout at anybody, it might surprise them — it shouldn't make them afraid. Also, I am not in the sort of ex-communication business. I cannot, nor would I choose to come between a man and God or between a man and his beliefs. I can ring a bell and hold out the book like the best Cardinal that you have ever seen — and it will have as much effect as you allow it to have.

Never forget, I am there, performing a function to the best of my ability. *I am there to bring about circumstances, to perhaps influence circumstances and perhaps to guide circumstances — by any and all means or methods at my disposal, whether it be asking you to do a three-day fast, or to put on a hula skirt and dance on the table.* The measure is how one creates the effect, and fortunately, in the Tradition, by any means, which may very often be entirely different from the outward appearance of the circumstance. I just leave with one final thing before I tell you another Nasrudin joke — and that is — and I can't force you to do it, because you must each examine your own experience — believe and understand that I know my function, and I do it very well.

You can all go away and ponder the next joke that I am going to tell you — but actually it is a joke and an end in itself because the meaning of it is self-evident. A man went to Nasrudin and said, "Nasrudin, you are a clever man and esoteric and so forth, show me God if you're so clever" — so Nasrudin, who was digging in his garden, picked up a stone and hit the man on the head. The man went off howling to the judge and complained. The judge called Nasrudin, and said "Nasrudin, you are a learned man, what an awful thing to do. He asked you a perfectly reasonable question, why can't you give him a reasonable answer?" And Nasrudin said, "What is he complaining about?" And he said, "He's complaining because you hit him on the head and he has a terrible pain and everything." Nasrudin said, "Well, if this man will show me the pain, then I will show him God."

BIBLIOGRAPHY

Rafael Lefort *The Teachers of Gurdjieff* Gollancz, London

Idries Shah *The Sufis* Octagon Press, London

Idries Shah *The Way of the Sufi* Octagon Press and Penguin Books, London

Al-Ghazzali *The Alchemy of Happiness* Octagon Press, London

Ernest Scott *The People of the Secret* Octagon Press, London

Idries Shah *Subtleties and Exploits of the Inimitable Mulla Nasrudin* Octagon Press, London

Rumi *The Mathnawi* Trans. Harold Nicholson, Luzac Books, London

Hafiz *The Diwan* Trans. Wilberforce Clarke, Octagon Press, London

Teachings of Hafiz Intro. Idries Shah, Octagon Press, London

Jami *Yusuf and Zulaikha* Octagon Press, London

The Rubaiyyat of Omar Khayamm trans Robert Graves and Omar Ali-Shah, Cassell, London

Aflaki *The Hundred Tales of Wisdom* translated and adapted by Idries Shah, Octagon Press, London

Saadi *Le Jardin de Rose*s *(Gulistan)* traduction Omar Ali-Shah, Editions Albin Michel, Paris (épuisé)

Four Sufi Classics: Jami's *Salaman and Absal,* and *The Abode of Spring (Bahariston),* Al-Ghazzali's *Niche for Lights,* Hakim Sanai's *The Way of the Seeker* Octagon Press, London

Amina Shah *The Assemblies of Al-Hariri* Octagon Press, London

The Sirdar Ikbal Ali-Shah *The Spirit of the East* Octagon Press, London

Kashiti, Husain Vaiz *Ahlaki Muhsini (Morals of the Beneficent)* (In preparation)

Affiri, abu *Philosophy of ibn ul Arabi*

Ali-Shah, *The Sirdar Ikbal, Islamic Sufism,* London, 1936

Ali-Shah, Omar *Garden of Roses of Sheikh Saadi Shirazi* (In preparation)